KEYS TO RAISING A DRUG-FREE CHILD

Carl E. Pickhardt, Ph.D.

BARRON'S

Cover photo by Photo Disc.

DEDICATION
To my wife, Irene, for her expert editorial help in the final stages of this manuscript, and to the Barbara Bauer Literary Agency for sticking with my writing over the long haul.

Material in this book is drawn from conducting workshops with parents and from counseling families about preventing, responding to, and recovering from what happens when a child abuses substances. Unless otherwise noted, all examples and quotes given are fictitious, created to illustrate a psychological point.

All inquiries should be addressed to:
Barron's Educational Series, Inc.
250 Wireless Boulevard
Hauppauge, New York 11788
http://www.barronseduc.com
Library of Congress Catalog Card No.: 99-23278
International Standard Book No.: 0-7641-0848-4

Library of Congress Cataloging–in–Publication Data
Pickhardt, Carl E., 1939–
    Keys to raising a drug-free child / Carl E. Pickhardt.
      p.   cm. — (Barron's parenting keys)
    Includes bibliographical references and index.
    ISBN 0-7641-0848-4
    1. Children—Drug use—United States. 2. Youth—Drug use—United States. 3. Drug abuse—United States— Prevention. 4. Parenting—United States. I. Title. II. Series.
HV5824.C45P53   1999
649'.4—dc21   99-23278
                                      CIP

PRINTED IN THE UNITED STATES OF AMERICA
9 8 7 6 5 4 3 2 1

CONTENTS

INTRODUCTION

"DRUGS ARE EMPTY FUN"

Parents fear at least *seven deadly experiences* that can damage or destroy their children's lives:

1. Victimization from violence
2. Accidental injury
3. School failure
4. Illegal activities
5. Sexual misadventures
6. Suicidal despondency
7. Drug and alcohol involvement

This book is about the last fear—the most powerful of the seven because when you eliminate drug and alcohol involvement, you can reduce the incidence of the other six. *The choice to use substances affects how other life decisions are made.*

No wonder most parents wish that the problems of substance use, abuse, and addiction would just disappear. Think of all the suffering that families would be spared! The availability and consumption of drugs and alcohol, however, is not going to vanish. Wishful thinking is no protection from the dangers that substances can create for children. Like it or not, alcohol and drugs are part of the society in which we live. They are embedded in our cultural fabric and play an active role in many people's daily lives. Legally and illegally sold to great profit in our marketplace, they create a persistent set of health and social problems that will not go away.

Of course, drugs are not simply a "problem" and nothing more. Today, as throughout human history, people have turned to naturally occurring and manufactured chemicals for medicinal, ceremonial, religious, and recreational purposes for the relieving and healing, mood and mind-altering effects these substances can offer. In this sense, times haven't changed because people haven't changed. *If drugs didn't have something positive to offer, human beings wouldn't keep taking them.*

In the culture of the United States today, however, there is a difference.

- There are more varieties of legal and illegal drugs available than at any time in human history.
- The sale of these substances generates unprecedented profits that support enormously powerful legitimate and underground sectors of our economy.
- The massive and persuasive national advertising of legal recreational drugs for adults encourages young people to act adult by participating in this use, often seeking out illicit drugs as well.

Ongoing surveys of young people's use of drugs and alcohol, like that conducted annually by the University of Michigan, continue to document how chemically active today's children are. About 50 percent of high school seniors, for example, report getting drunk on alcohol. College-age drinking, particularly binge drinking, only gets worse.

As for declaring "War On Drugs" by resolving to prosecute their illegal trafficking and consumption, this effort appears to help only a little because availability of these substances and appetite for their use both remain extremely high. *At most, making manufacture, sale, and use of drugs criminal may diminish some of the supply and demand, but has not and will not eradicate the problem.*

Perhaps what is most needed in those high-impact communities (extremely rich and extremely poor)—where, out of boredom from having too much or desperation from having too little, drugs are "all" that young people feel there is worth doing—is an increased variety of other choices. Social, spiritual, recreational, artistic, educational, service, and employment opportunities can sometimes provide healthy alternatives to the empty fun that substance use provides.

I believe the best way to protect young people is through preparing their parents to

- confront this social threat to children and not deny it
- educate their children about the risks of substances, and offer guidelines for safety should use occur
- educate themselves to recognize and helpfully respond when substance use is hurting their child and disrupting their family life
- employ preventive strategies to prepare children to live satisfying lives independent of (and not dependent on) the use of alcohol and drugs
- give children the coping tools, through instruction and example, to accept and work through *emotional pain as a normal part of human life*, not treating times of suffering as bad experiences that should be escaped by resorting to substances in order to feel better

It is my hope that this book gives parents some measure of help in achieving these objectives. Part One begins by examining four fundamental aspects of the substance use problem. Part Two describes various levels of destructive substance involvement. Part Three alerts parents to major influences on children's substance use. Part Four focuses on emotional states sometimes provoking substance use. Part Five examines developmental pitfalls in the stages of adolescence that can make a young person receptive to drugs. Part

Six suggests steps toward intervention when a child needs help. Part Seven discusses treatment alternatives. Part Eight outlines dimensions of family functioning that can be adversely affected by a child's substance use, and how healthy functioning can be recovered.

At the end of the book are common questions parents ask, the answers to which are not already covered in the body of the text; a list of suggested readings; the names of helpful support groups and organizations; and a glossary defining some terms that may be unfamiliar.

The Meaning of the Term "Drug-free"

Although the ready availability of substances is a harsh reality for children growing up today, raising "*a drug-free child*" is a realistic and worthwhile goal for all parents, whether this definition means

- raising children who never get involved with drugs and alcohol at all
- raising children who sometimes use but never, in their own and other people's judgment, get harmfully involved with drugs and alcohol
- raising children who become involved with these powerful substances to their personal cost, but, with help, recover healthy lives

Drug freedom may be a hard goal to achieve, but it is one on which the current and future well-being of every child depends. Throughout this text, one underlying key is continually emphasized: *communication*. I believe that the best hope parents have for growing a drug-free child is to talk and talk and talk to their son or daughter about the realities of substances and substance use, abuse, and addiction. This book provides parents with many ways to discuss this topic with their child.

1

DENIAL

THE ENEMY IN HIDING

No matter how disorganized their lives have become, children on substances do not usually self-refer for help. Instead, they appear brazenly untroubled by their destructive use. Why? The answer is *denial*.

- "I'm not acting any different than before."
- "You're just imagining things."
- "I don't have a problem."
- "It's no big deal."
- "I can handle it."
- "I can quit any time I want."
- "It's not affecting how I'm leading my life."
- "If it makes me feel good, how can that be bad?"
- "All my friends are doing it and they're okay, so I am too."

Denial is the intellectual act by which people block out the evidence of their senses—the existence of a past hurt, current problem, or potential danger in their lives. Substance abuse (where harmful choices are being made) and addiction (where dependency is established) are enabled by denial. In addition, lying to oneself and to others also supports destructive use: "The drugs you found in my room aren't mine. I was just keeping them for a friend." Where lying like this is conscious and deliberate, however, denial is done more unawares. On some level people know what they are doing, but on another they do not: "I was just driving after having a few beers; it's not like I was driving drunk."

In the following quotes taken from the Stephen F. Austin High School newspaper *Maroon*, September 14, 1998 story on binge drinking, the students interviewed don't quite see what they are saying.

- "I'm going to drink no matter what. We just have more fun when we drink."

- "I drove drunk because I needed to get home. It's really not as hard as everyone thinks; I mean it doesn't take a miracle to get you home."

- "Everyone's done it at least once. After the first bad experience, I'll quit. Besides, sixteen-year-olds don't die. It just doesn't happen."

- "I don't think drinking is a big deal. Sure everybody does it every weekend, but it's not out of control."

- "It would suck if something bad happened, but I'm not worried."

So, if the child is denying a problem with substances, who is going to admit it and seek the help that is needed? Parents seem like the logical next choice, except they are often in denial, too. Why? Because admission feels so threatening or painful that they become afraid.

- They may fear *personal guilt:* "What have we done wrong?"

- They may fear *public censure:* "What will friends and family think of us?"

- They may fear *social shunning:* "Suppose other people won't want anything to do with us, keeping their child away from ours?"

- They may fear *responsibility:* "Will our parenting be implicated in our child's use?"

- They may fear *repetition:* "How can I face having a drug-abusing child when having alcoholic parents was so bad?"

- They may fear *the necessity to change:* "Suppose we have to question or even give up our evening drinking to keep our child free from the desire to use (substances) at home?"

It is in consequence of fears like these that parents can develop denial of their own.

- "Our son swears he's not doing drugs, so we believe him."

- "Our daughter says it's the first time she's ever gotten drunk, and she's learned her lesson, so thank goodness she won't ever do it again."

- "We're just not the kind of family who would have a child involved with drugs."

- "Of course we recognize that there are problems, but it can't be drugs. It must be something else."

- "Skipping school and lying to us about it is just normal teenage misbehavior."

Denial doesn't prevent problems, it protects problems. Better for a parent to keep an open mind: "Problems with alcohol and drugs can happen to any child, *including my own.*"

The power of denial goes beyond initial blocking out. Denial by the child and by the parents delays early recognition of the problem and seeking help. *Admission takes time because denial must be overcome.* And when the problem is finally confronted, denial still delays full discovery because the child usually understates the scope of what has actually been going on, and parents usually underestimate the damage substance use has done.

What allows parents to overcome their denial? As more and more evidence of the problem accumulates, parents reluctantly, through a process of painful elimination of lesser possibilities, become convinced that what they have long dreaded and rejected is actually true. How else to explain why all their well-intended speeches and strategies have failed to stem the flow of misbehavior? The lies have continued, the promises have kept being broken, the troubles have mounted, the continuing crises have created constant stress, and, at last, a final misadventure becomes more than parents are willing to ignore. They "bottom out." They've had enough. They add up all the evidence again and reach an inescapable conclusion: their son or daughter is harmfully involved in alcohol or drugs. In the fight between admission and denial, honesty born of desperation finally wins out.

Because most denial is based on fear, admission is an act of courage. But now another fight is typically begun. Still in denial, the child resists what steps the parents are now prepared to take, and what help they are prepared to seek. *Denial is defended by resistance.* In the case of helping solve their child's problems with substances, there is no easy way out. It requires courageous and constant parental love.

One way to lessen parental predisposition to denial is to declare two fundamental equations *in*valid: *Parent = Child*, and *Problem = Person.*

Parent = Child

This first equation implies that performance of the child is a direct reflection of performance of the parent, and that adequacy of parenting is measured by success or failure of the child. Thus, when the child does badly, this equation implies that parenting is going badly, that bad parenting is responsible for the child's difficulty or misconduct. Enter the *guilt* and *shame* of parents unable to face the problem because they feel unable to face themselves: "We must have done wrong for our child to go wrong."

4

Break this equation and the tyranny of those twin emotions are broken. Parents can reduce their susceptibility to denial by *limiting their liability* for how the child acts. They can accept realistic limits about how much of their child's life they are actually able to control.

Parents only have a modest amount of influence over the course and conduct of their child's life. Consider *three basics they do not and never will control:*

1. Their child's inborn *characteristics* (by temperament a high risk taker)

2. The outside *circumstances* to which their child is exposed (a friend offers alcohol for the boy or girl to try)

3. The *choices* the child makes (to join the friend to see what getting drunk is like)

Problem = Person

This second equation also needs to be declared invalid because it implies that a *bad* problem = a *bad* person. No. Any child is infinitely larger than the sum of his or her problems, and parents must hold onto the broadest possible perspective, not losing sight of the positive when the negative occurs. Lose that perspective and give into the Person = Problem equation, and they will identify the child as "nothing but a problem." Then the child will do the same for himself or herself, and invaluable personal strengths and resources will be discounted and ignored, made unavailable for help in recovery. As one child angrily reminded his parents: "Drugs is not all I do! Addicted is not all I am!" And the child was correct.

The best defense against the problem of parental denial is for parents to cut themselves free from the implications of both equations and subscribe to the following statement:

Getting into trouble and having problems are a part of every child's growing up. They are not an indictment of the child or of the parenting that child receives. Making some bad decisions does not make the child a bad person or the mother or father a bad parent. Good parents have good children who will sometimes make bad choices in the normal trial-and-error process of growing up.

Some of those choices may involve substances because drugs and alcohol are part of every growing child's world in the United States today. When children choose their way into any kind of trouble, including that involving alcohol and drugs, the role of the parent is to help them take responsibility for these decisions, face their consequences, choose their way out, and learn from the adversity that was created.

2

⋀⋀⋀

ARRESTED DEVELOPMENT

HOW SUBSTANCE USE CAN INHIBIT HEALTHY GROWTH

The dangers of alcohol and drug involvement for children are not simply that, under its influence, they can make destructive, even deadly, choices. Most commonly, the cost is measured not in loss of life, but in *loss of competence* from failing to engage with the challenges that are part of a healthy growing up.

What challenges? Ultimately, they all have to do with learning how to acquire effectiveness, achieve autonomy, and nourish self-esteem through the affirmative choices one makes. Growth is a gathering of power from dependence in infancy to independence in adulthood, with young people feeling more empowered to manage on their own and to count on themselves in constructive ways.

Unfortunately, what tends to happen to young people as they begin substance use, go from substance use into substance abuse, or move from substance abuse into addiction, is that they increasingly disengage, instead of engage, with many challenges that life presents. In consequence, healthy development can become arrested.

To illustrate what is meant, consider two young people, X and Y. Both are seventeen years old, are the same sex,

7

come from comparable backgrounds, and have comparable experiences, except in one respect. From the age of twelve, X has been regularly abusing substances, but Y has not. Now contrast them across nine categories of choices—X more often electing to *disengage* from the demands of reality; Y more often electing to *engage* with those same demands.

X:		Y:
Breaks promises to self and others	(COMMITMENT)	*Keeps promises* to self and others
Doesn't finish what is started	(COMPLETION)	*Finishes* what is started
Doesn't maintain continuity of effort	(CONSISTENCY)	*Maintains* continuity of effort
Avoids dealing with painful situations	(CONFRONTATION)	*Encounters* painful situations
Lets impulse rule over judgment	(CONTROL)	*Lets judgment rule* over impulse
Disowns results of actions	(CONSEQUENCES)	*Owns results* of actions
Decides by default when deciding gets hard	(CLOSURE)	*Decides by hard choice* when deciding gets hard
Shuts up about or acts out hard feelings	(COMMUNICATION)	*Speaks up* about and talks out hard feelings
Gives up what has mattered to self and family	(CARING)	*Holds onto* what has mattered to self and family

Young people and adults recovering from substance abuse or addiction typically have a lot of catching up, and growing up, to do. To some degree, they have taken chemicals to disengage from the demands of reality in order to momentarily free themselves from normal constraints, challenges, and cares. So, in the case of the comparison made above, X may pay the following costs for deciding to disengage.

- By repeatedly breaking promises to self, X has *lost* some faith in his or her *capacity for self-reliance.*

- By repeatedly starting much but finishing little, X has *lost* some confidence in his or her *capacity to follow through and meet personal goals.*

- By repeatedly being unable to keep up a healthy daily regimen, X has *lost* some *capacity for self-care.*

- By repeatedly choosing to escape personal pain, X has *lost* some *capacity to tolerate and work through emotional hurt.*

- By repeatedly giving into the lure of immediate gratification, X has *lost* some *capacity to resist temptation.*

- By repeatedly denying the connection between bad choice and bad consequence, X has *lost* some *capacity for personal responsibility.*

- By repeatedly letting circumstances determine difficult decisions, X has *lost* some *capacity for mental toughness.*

- By repeatedly refusing to express hard feelings directly, X has *lost* some *capacity for open and honest communication.*

- By repeatedly betraying what has traditionally mattered, X has *lost* some *capacity to feel positively connected to self and family.*

So at the age of seventeen, maybe this X is functionally, in terms of intellectual and emotional maturity, about age fourteen. Assuming he or she can remain sober, there is a lot of self-esteem to be recovered and a lot of independence to be developed. In sum, this means that parents must *extend* their active parenting by providing their support for awhile longer and continuing to give their guidance, supervision, and structure to help the child catch up to his or her actual age.

What can parents say to keep encouraging their child to directly engage with the demands and challenges of life? They can offer some simple advice that, if consistently followed, may help shape that part of the child's growth over which he or she has some measure of choice.

1. "Keep your promises and agreements."

2. "Finish what you begin."

3. "Maintain what matters to you."

4. "Treat hurt feelings openly and honestly."

5. "Use good judgment to resist bad temptation."

6. "Own your bad decisions so you can learn from your mistakes."

7. "Learn to choose between hard choices, when hard choices are all you have."

8. "When you have hurts or problems, talk them out."

9. "Don't betray what you truly care about, or you will betray yourself."

Finally, there is a further cost, beyond arrested development, that some drug-abusing or addicted children may pay. From years of drug-induced incompetence at effectively dealing with normal challenges of growing up, a susceptibility to depression from *learned helplessness* may develop, with the young person losing confidence in self, in trying, and in optimism about life. (See Suggested Reading, Peterson et al.) In some cases, it's hard to tell if the young person is depressed from the developmental cost of using chemicals, or is using chemicals to manage painful feelings of depression, or is caught in a trap where both dynamics are in place, each worsening the effect of the other. *Drug abuse and addiction can both be seriously depressing.*

3

~~~~~~

SUBSTANCES OF CONCERN

THE INCREASING VARIETY

A ccording to one authority (see Suggested Reading, Schuckit, p. 26), there are over two hundred and fifty mood- or mind-altering (psychoactive) substances being sold in the legal and illegal marketplaces in this country today, and the variety continues to increase. Given this abundance, how are parents supposed to be adequately informed about every kind of substance, its effects and risks, and its warning signs of use? *Parents are not expected to be experts in pharmacology;* they are to have only a sufficient general awareness of the array of substances in their child's world to factor in the possibility of his or her use when unusual negative or destructive behavior occurs.

What Is a "Substance"?

Substances are chemicals that are smoked, inhaled, swallowed, injected, sniffed, absorbed, or inserted into the child's body, entering the bloodstream with varying degrees of rapidity, and ending up in the brain where they affect how the boy or girl feels, thinks, perceives, or acts.

Substances may be taken for a host of reasons. The primary motivation in repeated use, however, is to *repeat* the *effects* already experienced, and those effects vary with the substance used, how often it is used, the amount ingested, and the individual variation between people themselves. Thus, alcohol can make one person happy and another sad, one person congenial and another argumentative, and the same person at first animated and then drowsy with further use. In addition, to what degree alcohol is absorbed in the bloodstream also varies based on the person's weight, gender, eating habits, and time elapsed since the last drink. Thus, two beers in quick succession for a 100-pound woman on a crash diet will result in a higher blood alcohol level than for a 200-pound man after a full meal who has waited half an hour before opening up the second can.

Why Use Substances?

Although parents, by instruction and example, may want to take a position with their child that discourages use, they also need to be realistic about the many mood- and mind-altering payoffs that substances provide because among these may be the predictable effects that their child is seeking. For example, people take substances to:

- Enjoy company and increase status
- Avoid discomfort and escape problems
- Counteract boredom with excitement
- Induce a sense of pleasure or euphoria
- Get a sense of floating and detachment
- Create feelings of confidence and power
- Experience disorientation and confusion
- Satisfy a craving caused by previous use
- Get a glow on, mellow out, and relax
- Heighten alertness and stimulate sensation
- Perceive a nonusual reality
- Reduce tension and relieve pain
- Calm fear and allay anxiety

- Free up expressivity
- Stimulate productivity
- Lift depression

Every substance has transformative power—it can change a person's mood, it can alter a person's perception. Every substance can at least become psychologically addictive with repetition (compulsion to continue use despite problems caused), and many can become physically addictive (the body adjusts with craving, tolerance, and withdrawal). Every substance is also a poison—amount and frequency of use can have harmful, even lethal, effects. "Drug overdose is the method most frequently used in suicide attempts." (See Suggested Reading, Merck, p. 413.)

For parents, when it comes to forestalling their child's substance use, *the price of prevention is eternal vigilance.* They have to keep a close watch on their child's behavior and be willing to consider substance involvement when a change or choice for the worse by their son or daughter is not fully explained by the data at hand. What kinds of changes should parents look for?

- When smart kids make stupid decisions
- When good kids act bad
- When truthful kids lie
- When mindful kids can't remember
- When conscientious kids become indifferent
- When even-tempered kids develop mood swings
- When kids with little money have a lot to spend
- When capable kids fail
- When dedicated kids lose interest
- When communicative kids shut up

- When open kids become secretive
- When nice kids act mean
- When responsible kids act irresponsibly
- When reliable kids default on their agreements
- When motivated kids start not to care
- When careful kids act careless
- When obedient kids break rules and laws
- When focused kids have accidents
- When honest kids steal
- When healthy kids become rundown

None of these changes individually is a guarantee of substance use, but over time a pattern combining a number of these behaviors are cause for parental concern. (For more specific signs to look for, see Key 24.) *Preventive parenting requires keeping a protective lookout.* Look out for any possible use of substances that fall within the following categories.

Categories of Substances

There are many ways that experts categorize the different substances available. What follows is not a definitive list, but an effort to simply organize a number of systems into one.

1. *Depressants:* to sedate, to treat anxiety, to relax, to induce sleep, to relieve tension/worry
   - Alcohol (beer, wine, distilled spirits)
   - Barbiturates ("downers" like Nembutal and phenobarbital)
   - Tranquilizers (Valium, Librium, Thorazine)
   - Hypnotics (sleep aids)

2. *Narcotics:* to control pain
   - Opioids (prescription analgesics like morphine and codeine; heroin, which is illegal in this country but medicinally approved in some others)

3. *Inhalants:* to create giddiness, light-headedness, and confusion
   - Solvents (gasoline, paint thinner, correction fluid)
   - Gases (freon, nitrous oxide, aerosols)
   - Glues (nail polish, plastic cement, airplane glue)
   - Cleaning agents (spot remover, dry-cleaning fluid, degreaser)

4. *Psychedelics:* to induce a dreamy state, a floating feeling, perceptual distortion, heightened and abnormal sensations, exaltation, excitement
   - Cannabinols (marijuana, hashish, THC)
   - Hallucinogens (LSD, mescaline, psilocybin)

5. *Stimulants:* to increase alertness, reduce fatigue, lift depression, decrease appetite, speed up bodily processes and activity, enhance physical performance and well-being, create euphoria and grandiosity
   - Amphetamine ("uppers" like Benzedrine and Dexedrine)
   - Weight-reducing drugs (Dexatrim)
   - Methamphetamine (speed)
   - MDMA (Ecstasy)
   - Antidepressants (Elavil, Ritalin, Prozac)
   - Caffeine (coffee, cola, tea, NoDoz)
   - Cocaine (coke, crack)
   - Nicotine (cigarettes, cigars, pipes, snuff)

6. *Other:*

- Steroids (taken to increase muscle mass; aggressiveness and mood swings can also be induced)
- Ketamine or "K" (an animal anesthetic, taken as an inhibition-relaxing drug)
- Over-the-counter drugs (According to Schuckit, pp. 47–48—see Suggested Reading—some medications for sleep can contain antihistamines or anti-anxiety drugs; some medications for nasal congestion can have stimulant effect; some cough medications can contain alcohol; some anti-cough medications can have narcotic effects.)

Although there is no fixed developmental schedule for what ages children will try which drugs, readings suggest that inhalants ("huffing") tend to be a drug of choice for the very young; tobacco and alcohol come soon after; then come marijuana and other psychedelics; diet pills (stimulants) and steroids begin with mid-adolescent concern about body shape; and cocaine use is more likely to begin before heroin, which tends to begin around age eighteen. Speed, which tends to begin in the mid- to late-twenties, and prescription stimulant and depressant abuse are more common in adulthood.

The four most common substances abused by young people are inhalants, tobacco, alcohol, and marijuana. The latter three are most commonly abused by adults. Children who smoke cigarettes are significantly more likely to use other drugs and even more likely to drink heavily than non-smokers. *Two legal drugs do most of the killing*: "Smoking kills more people in the United States than any other drug, except alcohol." (See Suggested Reading, Schuckit, p. 373.)

In the culture we have created, the one that our children will grow up in, chemical self-medication is part of many people's daily way of life—to get started, to keep going, to stay healthy, to live longer, to feel better, to face adversity, to get work done, to reward effort, to unwind, to escape from care, to stop suffering, and to enable sleep. Whether with sugar, herbal remedies, caffeine, nicotine, alcohol, pot, uppers, downers, or whatever, people routinely self-administer chemicals to minister to their physical and psychological well-being. In the words of cartoonist Walt Kelly: "We have met the enemy, and they are us." *In a drug-filled culture, it is a great challenge to raise drug-free kids.*

4

‸‸

LEGAL CONSEQUENCES

WHAT TO TELL YOUR CHILD ABOUT THE LAW

I s it worth talking to your children about anti-drug laws, enforcement, and consequences for violation? After all, so the argument goes, if children are determined to use illicit substances, then concern for the law, or for risks from breaking it, is not likely to keep them from following through on their intent.

Perhaps this is true for the determined young user. For the child whose choice is wavering, however, such information can have a deterrent effect. The guideline for parents here is simply: *keep weighing in with what you want your children to know about substance use, and what you want them to do in response.* Parents who shut up are parents who give up, turning over influence to less reliable information offered by the child's peers. ("Nobody ever gets busted for smoking pot.") *At issue is helping children understand the legal framework regarding substances within the society in which they live.*

Begin by explaining to your children that in addition to whatever psychological and physical harm it can wreak in their lives, involvement with substances can also put them at legal risk. Caffeine, over-the-counter medications, prescription drugs from home, household glues and solvents, may all be within the law, but many other substances are not.

Alcohol and nicotine products, for example, are age restricted, whereas federal law prohibits anyone from trafficking in or using heroin or LSD, which are Schedule I substances according to the federal government's system for regulating dangerous drugs. Of the five schedules, Schedule I use is most tightly controlled, with the penalties for violations most severe. Schedule I drugs supposedly meet three criteria: they have a high potential for abuse, they have no currently accepted medical use, and they lack safety even under medical supervision.

Agree or not, *marijuana is currently federally designated Schedule I.* So if children choose to consider it no more than a harmless, recreational drug, they need to know that because of its current classification, involvement with marijuana is often treated as an extremely serious violation of the law. Prosecution of the federal violation sometimes takes precedence over state statutes that apply. In the past several decades, millions of people have been arrested for possession, use, and sale of marijuana—more than half a million in 1966 alone. Apparently, when a substance that people want is outlawed, some will risk becoming outlaws to get it, whereas others will not.

Along with their other duties, police officers are supposed to enforce local, state, and federal anti-drug laws. Most major urban police departments have special narcotic units that go after those who traffic in drugs. Anti-drug laws and enforcement of those laws are in place in all communities. In consequence, over half the convicts in federal prisons are convicted of drug or drug-related charges. *There is a vast anti-drug enforcement apparatus in place in this country today.*

Children need to understand that *ignorance is no protection from prosecution* when, for example, after being stopped for a moving violation, the sixteen-year-old is surprised to be charged with Minor In Possession for having an unopened can of beer in the car. "But I wasn't drinking!" he or she protests. That's not the point. The boy or girl was driving in possession. *Parents have the responsibility for informing their children about the law.*

Explaining the law does not mean arguing with the child about such questions as Do anti-drug laws actually deter use? Does making drug use criminal really make society a safer place? Does prohibition do more harm than good? Would legalizing drugs have greater social benefits?

Although answers to these questions are open to debate, the existence of anti-drug laws and their enforcement is not. It is a reality that children need to understand and accept. Therefore, parents should talk to their children about *three* kinds of violations and the consequences that can follow: *Possession, Use,* and *Sale* of prohibited substances.

Since there is variation in anti-drug laws between different cities and between different states, parents may want to check for more specifics with their local authorities. A separate jurisdiction that children need to be aware of are the public schools, most of which have anti-drug regulations in place, and procedures for suspending or expelling students for on-campus possession, use, or sale of substances. In addition, the penalties for selling drugs on or near school premises are usually significantly more severe than selling them elsewhere.

When a child is arrested as a *juvenile* (under eighteen years of age), the court proceeding is a hearing, not a trial, and the outcome, at least for a first offense, is usually probation. Successful completion of probation usually depends on meeting certain conditions, like attending school regularly, doing some community service, receiving some alcohol and drug education, and paying a fine.

Most offenses that have to do with *possession* are considered *misdemeanors*, acts of breaking the law that are usually not punishable by imprisonment, but if they are, imprisonment of less than a year. Offenses that have to do with *use*, particularly coupled with dangerous or destructive behavior like Driving Under the Influence or Driving While Intoxicated, can receive more serious penalties. *Sale* of drugs is usually a *felony* offense. *Felonies* are serious crimes punishable by more than a year of imprisonment, and in some cases (like murder) by death.

What to Say About Possession

Possession means having the drug on your person, in your school locker, in your car, or in your house. A child who keeps drugs in his or her room is putting the family at some legal risk because now parents have banned substances within their home. The act of buying drugs for use itself often puts the child in contact with some level of criminal element that may add significant social danger to the existing risk. In addition, although possession (of marijuana, for example) is usually treated as a misdemeanor, multiple arrests for possession, or for possession of a significant amount, can be treated as a felony offense.

If the child is at a party where people are using illegal drugs, even if he or she is not using, everyone may be arrested. Those children who are intoxicated, are in control of the drugs, or live on the premises are at higher risk of conviction. A child needs to know that simply being around drugs can get him or her in trouble with the law. In addition, there are civil forfeiture laws that empower police to seize a person's car, for example, when arresting a driver in possession of illegal drugs.

Obtaining and using a fake ID, or loaning or borrowing a real one to buy cigarettes or alcohol, are two offenses in one—falsifying identity and possessing a forbidden substance. Lending one's license to underage others is also against the law.

What to Say About Use

The jeopardy of use partly depends on knowing what you're using. When buying street drugs, the child has no way of verifying exactly what is being sold at what strength or mixed with what. So, *let the buyer beware.* Beyond this concern, however, is the matter of *influence*—the effects of impaired judgment on behavior, particularly when driving a car. Automobile accidents involving drugs or alcohol are a leading killer of adolescents today.

In recent years, Driving While Intoxicated (DWI) and Driving Under the Influence (DUI) have received increasingly severe penalties in most states. Over and above the assessment of liability for any damage done, a young person will usually face loss of license, a fine, community service, court-ordered substance abuse counseling, and perhaps some jail time. Police can stop a young person on suspicion (seeing erratic driving, for example), administer a *field sobriety test* to estimate if he or she has normal use of mental and physical faculties, administer a *breath test* to estimate blood alcohol level (needs to be less than .08 or .10, depending on the state), and, if those are failed, take the young person in for a blood or urine test to confirm the state of intoxication. Refusing to take a requested test usually works against the child in the eyes of the law.

Increasingly, in both private and public sectors, employees are subject to urinalysis drug testing whether use is suspected or not. Failure to pass that test can jeopardize employment. The most common illegal drug turned up by these tests is marijuana, since its use is so widespread—the third most popular drug in the United States after alcohol and nicotine. Days after any psychoactive effect has worn off, presence of the drug in one's physical system can be detected, and that detection can be used as grounds to recommend suspension, termination, or treatment.

As for mixing substances and foreign travel, adolescent-age children on trips abroad need to know their increased legal and other risks from using substances.

- To be drunk, high, or wasted in a foreign country can offend local customs, violate local laws, and increase the likelihood of social and sexual victimization.

- To be arrested for illegal use in a foreign country means being subject to that country's anti-drug laws, including possible long-term imprisonment. Being an American citizen is no protection. *The local United States consulate does not have the authority to get American offenders out of jail.*

- To be discovered transporting an illegal substance over a country's border, even if ignorant of the contents of the package that someone asked another person to carry as a favor, can get that person into the most severe legal trouble of all.

What to Say About Sale

Sometimes young people who get into selling drugs (often to finance their own use) will mistakenly trust their customers not to turn against them and turn them in. What these sellers forget is that what they are selling is evidence against themselves. So, *let the seller beware.* Parents can tell their child that possession can get you in trouble, use can get you in more trouble, but *selling—which is a felony—can get you in the most trouble of all.* And, if the seller doesn't pay his or her supplier, rough justice may follow.

What to Say About Responsibilities

Should the child get arrested for any kind of anti-drug law violation, it is generally in the boy or girl's best interest to experience some negative consequences for the choice he or she made. Given the vagaries of the law, parents may want to consult or retain an attorney to get appropriate legal advice, but the child should be responsible for paying some of that expense, be party to all legal consultations, and be present at all hearings.

Finally, parents need to make their own social assessment about likely treatment by the legal system. If they have cause to believe that their child has not or will not be fairly treated by the law because of prejudice or discrimination built into the criminal justice system, they need to factor in this heightened risk. They may feel that for the same drug offense (possession of cocaine, for example) suspicion would be more likely, enforcement more harsh, and sentencing more severe for an African-American male than for an Anglo female. If parents believe bias of any kind is likely, they need to communicate this increased jeopardy to their child, and to get legal representation to ensure equitable treatment should their son or daughter get arrested.

5

~~~~~~

ABSTINENCE

RISKS FROM NOT EVEN USING

"Everybody does it, even grown-ups!" is a very common explanation that young people give to justify their substance use. Parents need to reply: *"Not everybody uses substances."* For example, according to a recent University of Michigan survey of drug use by high school seniors, although almost half had tried marijuana, *slightly over half had not*. As for grown-ups, as much as a third of our adult population abstain from any recreational use of substances at all. So, if students choose to be abstinent, they have a lot of company.

To follow this path, however, particularly in high school, there are usually two social costs to pay. Either they must appear *odd person out* at many parties for choosing not to use in a situation where some degree of drinking and drug use are the norm, or they must avoid attending parties where substances are likely to be present. Fortunately, what many of these young people discover is that there are, in fact, many abstinent others like themselves who also enjoy getting together without the need or desire to depend on substance use in order to have fun.

Although the bias of this book is in favor of children abstaining from drug and alcohol use, *remaining "drug-free" is not complete protection from the harm substances can do.*

This is the longest Key in the book because there are a number of significant problems, often overlooked by parents, that are associated with abstinence:

- Experiential ignorance from not using
- Coping with other people's use
- Being the designated driver
- Being unmindful of prescriptive medication
- Becoming codependently involved in a friend or loved one's use (see Key 10)

Experiential Ignorance from Not Using

In the majority of cases, a young person's abstinence is not going to last forever. By the end of adolescence, more young people than not have experienced some degree of substance use, particularly with nicotine, alcohol, and marijuana. "Before their high school graduation, over 90 percent of adolescents have consumed alcohol." (See Suggested Reading, Schor, p. 51.)

Parents can, however, at least play for delay, trying to persuade their young son or daughter to put off first-time substance use until he or she is older. *Research studies suggest that the later substance use begins, the lower the likelihood that abuse or addiction will occur.* The eighteen-year-old, for example, may have more maturity and confidence than the immature, insecure early adolescent, who is often ruled by impulse, rebellion, and a defiant sense of invulnerability to danger.

Abstinence, then, is a good choice for parents to encourage a child to make; however, it can also create a dilemma. If their high-school-age child doesn't use substances, how is he or she going to learn to manage them should some degree of use occur when the boy or girl is older? For example, do parents want to send off to college a high school senior who is planning to join a fraternity without his having any firsthand knowledge about alcohol? In this case, *experiential ignorance* may cause the young man to miscalculate what dose of alcohol to take because he does not recognize the signs of his own intoxication, and does not know his own tolerance enough to set safe drinking limits. At the fraternity initiation, where drinking to get drunk, competitive drinking, challenge drinking, and binge drinking are often encouraged, he may put himself at harmful risk—at worst, of life-threatening acting out or even of alcoholic poisoning. *For both fraternity and sorority students, the self-reported incidence of binge drinking is far higher than for nonmembers,* according to a 1997 study conducted at the Harvard School of Public Health (*The Adelphian,* Winter 1999, p. 12).

Just as permissiveness is no protection, so prohibition (from parents or from self) is no preparation. What the young person doesn't know (about the dangers of mixing different types of alcohol, for example), or what he thinks he knows that isn't so (taking different substances at the same party is safe because they don't interact with each other, for example), can get him in a lot of trouble.

In order to counteract the naiveté that simple abstinence can bring, parents need to support *informed abstinence*—helping the child learn about the experience he or she is currently missing. *Abstinence does not have to mean ignorance.* Parents can legitimize the topic of substance use in family conversation so the child feels permission to talk about substance use in his or her world, and to ask questions when there is a need to know. Parents can try to provide what good information they have, editorializing about harmful substance use that is reported in the child's world without condemning the users and, thus, shutting the child's disclosures down. Parents are there to explain, not to judge. They can comment on the risks as they understand them and the warning signs to watch out for, and suggest guidelines for safe and responsible use if they know of any.

Because growing children learn both directly from their own experience and vicariously through the experience of others, parents can also inform their child's awareness by discussing some of their own youthful involvement with substances. Many fathers and mothers who have some early history with drugs or alcohol, however, are reluctant to share this information. They worry about undercutting the abstinence they are advocating by admitting their own past use.

They fear the child saying: "Well, if you did, then why shouldn't I?" But this risk needs to be weighed against a benefit. Parents often have a cautionary tale to tell, and they are extremely powerful informants. What they may lose in consistency ("Do like we say, not how we did") they may gain in credibility. In response, the child may well think: "My parents really know what they are talking about."

For example, parents might disclose:

- *When they used:* "I first tried pot when I was twelve years old, too young to know what I was getting into."
- *Why they used:* "Some popular friends of mine were doing it, so I went along in order to be cool."
- *What felt good about it:* "I was part of the gang, and everything felt mellow because smoking pot made me feel like nothing mattered and I didn't have to care."
- *What felt bad about it:* "The more I smoked, the more afraid I got of being caught; the more distrustful I became, the more I thought everyone was out to get me."
- *What they regret:* "Smoking dope caused me to give up things that had really meant a lot, and lying about it kept me really distant from my parents."
- *What they learned:* "I couldn't keep up my grades and keep smoking pot."

- *What happened when they gave it up:* "I was able to stop spinning my wheels; I started remembering better, slowly got my concentration back, and my life started going in a direction I cared about again."

Coping with Other People's Use

Simply because a child remains abstinent does not mean that he or she can always keep social company with friends and acquaintances who also abstain. Because it is a drug-filled world young people live in, parents need to talk with abstinent children about how to take care of themselves around other people's use.

The first piece of advice: *"Do not knowingly ever put yourself at the effect of someone else's dangerous drug or alcohol-influenced behavior."* The good friend a child can trust when sober can become extremely untrustworthy when drunk, stoned, wasted, or high. The change in outlook, mood, expression, and decision making can be dramatic. Drugs and alcohol can make that person less inhibited, more self-centered, less reliable, more impulsive, less in touch with reality, more attracted to risk taking, less able to reason, more combative, less caring about consequences, and more irresponsible. "I thought I knew him, but I was wrong. He became a different person, a different personality. And he was playing by a whole new set of rules. Only the game was serious. Someone was fixing to get hurt."

Although parents don't want their abstinent children to be at the mercy of this kind of behavior when just hanging around, on dates, at social gatherings, or at parties, drugs and alcohol often manage to show up. Therefore, children have to be responsible for evaluating the substance use around them, continually monitoring other people's consumption in terms of their physical state, emotionality, capacity for judgment, and decisions being made. Parents may want to consider suggesting the following set of guide-lines—*the five Rs*:

- Don't try to *reason* with someone who is adversely drug or alcohol affected (trying to explain that following the law does matter, for example) because there is no normal thinking person home.

- Don't try to *restrain* others' behavior (trying to persuade them that they have had enough, for example) because they are likely to resent the interference you provide, and rather than stopping them you end up starting a fight.

- Don't take *responsibility* for their behavior (blaming your-self for what they did or said, for example) because you only divert them from owning bad choices they have made.

- Don't try to *rescue* or protect them from consequences they have caused (bailing them out of trouble, for example) because you keep them from learning the hard lessons bad experience has to teach.

- Don't try to *recover* them (attempting to keep them from using again, for example) because that is ultimately out-side of your control.

Finally, tell your children that you do not want them ever to feel trapped in a drug- or alcohol-affected social situation in which they feel they have no escape. As parents, you want them always to have the power to leave when staying poses danger. Therefore, if they are too distant to walk away, do not have a car to drive away, or cannot be safely driven by someone else, make sure that they always carry emergency money for a taxi or other transportation, and that they know they can always call parents for an emergency pickup—no questions asked at the time, discussion to follow later, but no punishment given.

The Designated Driver

Designating a driver is a good rule, on the face of it. For safety's sake, have one teenager among a group of drinking friends take responsibility for remaining abstinent so he or she can do the driving to the party (because some young people imbibe some "social courage" before they go) and the driving home (because even a single drink can to some degree impair normal coordination and judgment). Parents don't want their child driving when he or she is drug or alcohol affected, nor do they want their child accepting transportation by someone who is drunk or high. After all, "Approximately 60 percent of all teenage drivers . . . who die in car accidents have been drinking . . . In fact, *alcohol-related accidents are the leading cause of death among 15- to 24-year-olds*, according to the Department of Health and Human Services." (See Suggested Reading, Zeigler Dendy, pp. 170–171.)

As a strategy for preventing drunk driving, creating the role of designated driver is double edged—a solution that comes with its own set of problems. Most obviously, at the same time it gives one teenager peer authorization to abstain, it also gives his or her companions implied permission to freely drink and use drugs because they are now relieved of transportation responsibility. Less obvious is what this designation does to the sober driver.

If it's not safe driving drunk, and it's not safe being driven by someone who's drunk, it's still not safe, even though the driver is sober, chauffeuring around a bunch of high or drunken friends. How is the designated driver supposed to control the car when rowdy passengers are all riotously acting out of control? (The safest number of drunk or wasted friends to drive is usually *one*.) If a passenger has an adverse reaction to "some pill" she was given after she'd been drinking, who is responsible for making that evaluation and getting help? (When in doubt, the designated driver may want to drive to the nearest emergency room to find out.)

Concerns and questions such as these make it necessary for parents to set some limits on safety and responsibility for their child when he or she is going to be the designated driver.

1. *"For safety's sake:* only agree to drive those people who are in a condition to be safely driven. If they are not, see if you can arrange other safe transportation—calling a taxi, their parents, or even us."

2. *"For responsibility's sake:* understand that you are not held accountable for their substance use, the affects of that use upon them, or the decisions they make when under the influence. Your primary responsibility is to keep yourself abstinent for the evening and provide sober transportation consistent with your own safety."

3. *"For awareness sake:* understand that most designated driving takes place at night when there are more drivers operating under the influence of substances than during the day—which is also one good reason to be extremely cautious driving late at night."

Being Unmindful of Prescriptive Use

It is important for young people to understand that just because someone abstains from *alcohol* or *recreational drugs*, he or she is not necessarily substance-free. Many young people take responsibly prescribed psychoactive medication to help them cope with a variety of physical conditions (pain, for example), behavioral problems (impulsivity, for example), or psychological states (depression, for example). There are medically sound reasons for taking these prescriptions, some over a sustained period of time. What the child needs to understand, however, is that *while on this regimen, he or she is not abstinent.* The boy or girl is "on drugs." Therefore, parents (if possible, with the prescribing physician's assistance) may want to recommend certain precautions to the child.

- "Do not independently self-regulate the amount or frequency of prescription use, because these drugs have a high potential for abuse, and in addition there can be a risk of adverse affects or even overdose."

- "It is particularly important, while taking these drugs, that you do not mix this medical use with the recreational use of alcohol or other drugs. The effects of prescriptive medication (tranquilizers, for example) can be amplified by additional substance use (taking another depressant like alcohol, for example), and the interaction can be dangerous in unpredictable ways."

- "Do not share or sell these medications to curious friends."

Parents need to remember, and need to remind their child, that *in a drug-filled world, abstinence is not a complete safeguard from the destructive effects of substances.*

6

‸‸

EXPERIMENTAL USE

CURIOSITY CAN HURT

Before parents can constructively discuss drug experimentation with their child, they need to explain one significant dimension of all drugs: their inherent danger.

The Danger of Drugs

Consider the dictionary definition of *poison*: "A substance . . . that in suitable quantities has properties harmful or fatal to an organism when it is brought into contact with or absorbed by the organism." (*Webster's Third International.*)

One way to describe any drugs, prescription or otherwise, is: *poisons with a purpose*. The *purpose* is to gain a desired medical or recreational effect. The *poison* is undertaking some degree of risk that chemical harm will be done. Because of its dual nature, any drug should be taken carefully. The user should be mindful that taking it for any purpose always involves a gamble of risking the poisonous potential of an adverse reaction for the therapeutic or pleasurable possibility of the desired effect.

If children, in service of denial, refuse to believe that all drugs have a possible downside, show them the warning labels attached to any over-the-counter or prescription drugs that routinely list possible side effects to beware. Then explain that although in general the beneficiaries far outweigh the casualties, thousands of people a year die from adverse reactions to prescription drugs, those side effects (allergic and otherwise) responsible for this fatal outcome. Who knows how many people actually fall casualty to unregulated street drugs each year?

No drug is 100 percent safe. The problem with psychoactive drugs (those taken for mood- and mind-altering effect) is a kind of triple jeopardy.

1. As with all drugs, adverse reactions are always possible.

2. Particularly with narcotics (pain killers), stimulants (uppers), and depressants (downers), there is a heightened possibility of physical addiction.

3. As a result of being in a psychologically affected state, the risk of unwise decision making is also increased, particularly when recreational drugs are added to prescription use.

Experimentation

It is healthy for children to experiment. Rooted in curiosity to discover the unknown and try out new experiences, experimentation is essential for learning, development, and growth.

It is normal for children, as they leave childhood and enter adolescence (usually between the ages of nine and thirteen) to start thinking about experimenting with substances. By mid-adolescence, the majority of fifteen-year-olds have tried cigarettes. By late adolescence, the vast majority of eighteen-year-olds have tried alcohol. To make matters worse, use tends to beget further use. The incidence of marijuana use, for example, is far greater among young people who already smoke and drink than those who do not. *In a drug-filled world, most children give some drugs a try.*

When parents discover that their child has been experimenting with substances, they need to ask themselves an important question: Is experimenting really what they have discovered? When the eleven-year-old solemnly declares: "It's the first time, I was just curious, and I won't do it again," parents need to weigh this statement carefully for truth.

In many cases, *admission of first-time use really means first-time caught*. The child is lying to cover up previous use. Therefore, parents need to reassess the last six months of their child's life to see if suspicious or unusual behavior occurred (tardies for first period in school, for example), or if circumstances similar to those surrounding the experimentation have happened before (there had been frequent overnights with a friend with whom the "experimental use" occurred, for example). The price for helping keep their child drug-free is the same for preserving any significant freedom: constant watchfulness.

"I don't huff glue that much. I just experiment with it on the weekends." No. *Multiple trials of the same substance constitutes a pattern of use*, and that is how it should be treated. For the child whose experimentation is likely to encourage further using, parents can educate about risk, increase supervision, reevaluate social freedom, restrict social contact, reinforce demands for responsibility, and consider the possibility of getting outside counseling help to evaluate the danger in what may be going on.

Experimentation Is Not All Bad

Experimentation with substances does not *always, automatically, and inevitably lead to recreational use, abuse, or addiction*. It can also lead to *abstinence*. Curious to find out what marijuana is like, for example, the young person tries it only to discover that "it didn't do anything for me," or, for whatever reason, he or she didn't enjoy the experience. So now, the boy or girl has no particular interest in using it again, in all likelihood continuing life free of that particular drug in the future.

Therefore, rather than panic at experimentation and assume much worse is yet to come, parents are better advised to ask the child about the experience. What was it like? Having tried it, what has the child learned from using the drug? A child who will openly discuss these two questions with parents is often one who is unlikely to get hung up on that drug because he or she now has no significant investment in further use.

Guidelines for Experimentation

If parents have any reason to believe that, despite their wishes and their warnings, experimentation is likely to occur, then they may want to consider giving that dreaded double message: "For all the reasons we have told you, we do *not* want you to experiment; but if you do, here are some precautions to take that might keep you from harm." *This preparation for doing what parents do not want the child to do is not permission. It is protection.* It is based on their realistic assessment of what the child is likely to do. And it begins with a statement about the nature of experimentation itself.

- "*Experimentation invites the unexpected.* It is like saying, 'Let's see what happens when . . .' You are deliberately risking an unknown experience in which unanticipated outcomes are expected to occur."

- "*Go slowly.* It's your body, it's the only one you get, so go at your own rate. If you're drinking, sip don't gulp, and keep about an hour between drinks that you limit to two. Don't feel you have to keep up with other people's use. Don't accept dares when it comes to use. Don't compete with other people to see who can use the most."

37

- *"Don't mix different kinds of substances.* And don't mix any substance use with other risk-taking behavior."

- *"Be aware of what you are taking.* If you get in difficulty from substance use and do not know what the substance was, timely help becomes harder to give."

- *"Make sure of your surroundings and your companions*—that the first are safe and the second can be trusted."

- *"Don't use under pressure from friends,* because true friends don't pressure you to use."

- *"Don't use to escape from unhappiness or pain,* because you risk reducing your tolerance for normal pain, and may make yourself feel worse at the time or later."

- *"Take responsibility for your experimentation* by monitoring your reaction to what you take. Let a little effect be enough to see what the substance is like. Don't feel you have to totally 'lose it' to get the full experience."

- "Remember, *with some substances experimentation (first-time use) can be fatal*—like trying to get drunk on antifreeze."

- *"A successful experiment is finding out what you wanted to know* without doing yourself or anybody else any harm."

7

RECREATIONAL USE

MODERATION AND MONITORED EFFECTS

I f experimentation is an act of curiosity—the *sampling* of a substance to discover the mental and physical effects it can create, recreational use has do with deciding to enjoy those effects again. *Freedom from negative experience (tension)* or *freedom for positive experience (disinhibition)* are the common goals. Using for enjoyment, however, is qualified by a restraint: *moderation.* Parents need to talk with the child, who has now begun a pattern of occasional or regular recreational use, about what constitutes moderate use.

What Is Moderation?

Perhaps the easiest way to describe moderation to their child is to do so in terms of its components. For use to remain moderate, some of the following criteria usually need to be met.

- Using with no observable harmful effects to self or others in the eyes of self or others. *Lack of moderation:* "I fell down because I was feeling woozy."

- Using so that normal rules for one's own appropriate conduct and standards of caring are not violated, creating cause for regret. *Lack of moderation:* "I said some things I wish I hadn't."

- Using so that afterward the person has full and accurate recollection of one's personal behavior. *Lack of moderation:* "Parts of last night I can't exactly remember."

- Using so that it is *not* done at a time or in a way that is disruptive of the person's important commitments or obligations. *Lack of moderation:* "Starting the day with a joint, it's hard to get to class on time."

- Using so that the amount of substance consumed is not more than was wanted or intended. *Lack of moderation:* "At some point, I just lost track of how much I was taking."

- Using so no pattern of habituation is established that dictates subsequent use whether the person thinks it is a good idea or not. *Lack of moderation:* "The main reason I did it again was because I had done it before."

- Using so that no increase in consumption is required to get the same desired effect. *Lack of moderation:* "It takes taking more to get a buzz on."

- Using substances that are amenable to the restraints of moderate use. *Lack of moderation:* " I felt like I could do anything, and I could do it forever!"

This last criterion is very significant because by definition it *excludes* the recreational use of stimulants, most depressants, sedatives, inhalants, and hallucinogens. Moderate use of alcohol is possible, and perhaps marijuana (although this seems to be more open to debate). Any recreational use of the other substances—speed, cocaine, heroin, LSD, solvents, for example—is probably not possible, given the power of their chemical effects.

Moderate use means using without causing problems for oneself or others. With *frequency* of use, *amount* of substance used, and *potency* of substance used, chances for moderation diminish and the likelihood of problems increase.

Monitored Use

Having given their child some guidelines in what constitutes moderation, parents still need to add one more restraint that characterizes recreational use. Not only is it done in moderation, but it is *monitored*. Tell the child that he or she is responsible for tracking the warning effects of excess substance use on both mind and body, eight tracks in all.

1. *Physical:* feeling unsteady, uncoordinated, clumsy, sick, very warm or very cold, agitated, tense. "I couldn't get my body to do what I told it to."

2. *Visual:* hard to focus, blurred vision, loss of significant detail, extremely drowsy or unable to close eyes at all. "I had a hard time telling which side of the road I was driving on."

3. *Verbal:* becoming uncharacteristically silent or talkative, slurring words, repeating sentences, incoherent speech. "Afterward, people told me they couldn't understand a word I was saying."

4. *Attitudinal:* becoming sentimental, sarcastic, argumentative, hostile. "All I wanted to do was pick a fight."

5. *Mental:* losing train of thought, becoming more confused or opinionated, obsessively fixated on a single, often painful, issue. "All I could think about was the breakup and how unfair that was."

6. *Emotional:* feelings becoming more intensified and extreme in response to ordinary events—elation or despair, hilarity or disgust, indifference or fear, omnipotence or helplessness. "I felt so scared, I just wanted to run away."

7. *Auditory:* not able to attend and listen, missing out on what is said, hearing voices when no one is speaking, not able to follow conversation, tuning others out. "I couldn't tell when people were talking to me."

8. *Perceptual:* ordinary reality becomes distorted, unrealistic, or fantastic. "It was like living in a crazy dream."

Awareness and responsibility are the keys to recreational use: using in moderation and continually monitoring effects that would signify excess use. Safe recreational use means consuming so that the first part of the brain affected by alcohol or drugs, the part that controls reasoning and judgment, is not impaired to the point it can no longer safely monitor use.

Impairment

Impairment occurs when two important risk inhibitors—judgment and reasoning—cease to function normally or are ignored. It happens, for example, when driving under the influence of alcohol (altered judgment) diminishes eye focus, side vision, night vision, and visual acuity. Or when the dreamy state induced by marijuana use slows reaction time and other motor abilities. It occurs, for example, when the young person miscalculates how much he or she is drinking (faulty reasoning) by forgetting that a 12-ounce can of beer can have as much pure alcohol as a 1.5-ounce shot of whiskey, acting as if drinking multiple beers is not the same as drinking "hard liquor." Parents can explain: *effectively monitoring use takes retaining one's capacity for normal judgment and reasoning.*

Finally, parents can add one last component of monitored use: *their intention to be involved in the monitoring process.* "Even though we have told you we don't want you to use, should you tell us or should we discover that you are, one consequence (*in addition to some temporary loss of freedom*) will be discussing exactly what happened. We will want you to think with us about why it happened, what protective decisions you made on this occasion, what risks you may have placed on yourself, and what you have learned from this experience that you didn't know before about how to safely take care of yourself should you use again. The restriction will remain in force until we have talked all this out."

Bad Decisions

Increasingly, the substance-abusing child becomes prone to making bad decisions that get the boy or girl into undeniable trouble.

- *For the sake of substance use,* he or she may rob money from family, sell drugs to friends, or steal beer from a convenience store, for example.
- *In the company of substance-abusing friends,* he or she may cut school or compete in acts of daring that lead to mishaps, for example.
- *Under the influence of substances,* he or she may have a driving, boating, swimming, or hunting accident, for example. (Fifteen- to twenty-year-olds are the age group most likely to be involved in alcohol-related traffic deaths.)
- *Giving up impulse control to substances,* he or she may not only give in to unwanted sex, but do so irresponsibly, using no protection against possible pregnancy or sexually transmitted disease, including HIV infection, for example. (Because so many high-risk sex experiences are drug or alcohol affected, *one of the best contraceptions is sobriety.*)

It is when *evidence of abuses* like these occur, that parents resort to hard loving—willing to act enemy to their child's self-destructive impulses for his or her best interests. Allowing the bad consequences from bad choices to be felt, they do not rush in and fix the problem, soften the trouble, or rescue the child from the lessons of responsibility that harsh reality has to teach. Now they begin to revise the terms on which the child lives with them at home.

Turning Back Abuse—Taking a Restrictive Stand

When substance abuse causes the child to suspend caring, act harmfully to self or others, and abuse freedoms that have been given, then parents need to place a tighter family structure around the child by *taking a restrictive stand*. Enforcing this new system of rules and expectations, they can expect some resentment and resistance and some increased argument and conflict for awhile. What they are looking for from their child is not approval or appreciation, but *consent*—going along with the regime they now impose.

Specifically, what kinds of restraints are commonly involved?

- No substance use of any kind will be allowed, and random drug testing can be expected at any time. Any violation of this zero-tolerance rule and other new restrictions will only delay future freedom until infractions are worked off.
- No discretionary money will be given.
- No driving will be allowed.
- No parties will be attended.
- Restitution will be paid for any thefts or other damages that have occurred.
- All allowable social arrangements will be double-checked by parents to substantiate truth.
- Social contact with drug-using friends outside of school is now forbidden.
- Household chores will be completed without complaint, in a timely and satisfactory manner, and personal space shall stay picked up, open for parental inspection at any time.
- Schedule and curfew permissions parents give depend on those agreements being kept.
- Present schoolwork will be completed, and past schoolwork will be made up.
- Attendance at family functions will be required.

- Money from any part-time job will be banked for the child, or the job given up.
- Acceptable language within the family will be insisted upon.

"These restrictions," explain the parents, "are in force until further notice, which doesn't mean forever, but until you begin to act in a more constructive manner at home, at school, and out in the world. Your freedom is only being reduced until solid evidence of more responsible conduct returns." In addition, more time with positive influences may be demanded—with extended family, with a regular exercise program, and with attending church, joining the youth group, or even meeting with an adult friend of the family who agrees to mentor the child for awhile.

Parents are not expecting 100 percent compliance with this new regime, only enough consent to cause the child to begin reshaping his or her attitude and judgment. Behavior change does not happen overnight. Parents must take their stand and give the child time to adjust. Regained caring and the making of better choices are the goals when turning back abuse, *and parents must recognize and appreciate (reward) all progress that they see.*

At this juncture, when the relationship between parents and child is often embattled, family counseling can be extremely helpful to talk and work out the adjustments being made (see Key 28). The cause for the battle being fought is an issue particularly dear to an adolescent's heart: *self-control.* Parents are taking a restraining stand to help the child recover responsible conduct after the boy or girl has lost to drugs control of caring and judgment.

Another definition of substance abuse is, in fact, exactly that: *when loss of responsible self-control occurs as a func-*

tion of losing control to drugs. At this point, risk of losing control in other areas of life dramatically increases: driving under the influence, unwanted and unprotected sexual acting out, breaking the law, acting on destructive impulse, overdosing, school failure, and accidental injury. So parents are not just opposing their son or daughter's involvement with drugs; they are concerned about a far larger issue of *safety,* and they should say so: "We are not simply fighting against your use of drugs, we are fighting for your life."

If after three months of their *consistently* maintaining a restrictive stand, the substance-abusing child still refuses to relinquish any of his or her self-destructive ways, then parents may want to consider the possibility of committing their son or daughter to an out-patient or in-patient drug treatment program (see Key 29).

When parents have done all they can within the family to stay the course of substance abuse and their efforts have proven not enough, then resorting to such external program help may be the best next choice. If the child refuses to go along with this decision for treatment, then a more dire choice can be presented: "Either attend treatment, or go live in a youth facility (of our choosing) for children unable to consent to family rules at home," or (if the child is over the age of seventeen) "make arrangements to live elsewhere, relying on your own self-support." *Sometimes it takes having to face the harsh demands of independent living to sober up and turn around the substance-abusing child.*

9

ADDICTION

ENTRAPMENT AND SELF-DEFEAT

The only reason taking a restrictive stand with a substance-abusing child can work is because parents consistently enforce the new regimen, and the child reluctantly conforms to what they have decreed. They can't force the child to obey because they can't control the child's choices. They can only influence those choices by the family structure they impose and the consequences they apply to decisions that are made. The child's compliance is an act of consent. To some extent, he or she agrees to go along with what they want. If, after several months of taking a restrictive stand, the child shows no signs of consent, then the problem may not be abuse. It may be addiction.

Although it is appropriate to take a restrictive stand with the addicted child as well, parents need to understand that compliance will usually be much harder to achieve because the substance-dependent child has much less power of consent over use. Psychological or physical dependency has now become so strong that it often overwhelms his or her personal choice. Instead of the child seeming in control of the substance (as in experimentation, recreational use, and abuse), now reliance on the substance seems to have taken control of the child. From living and using, the child is now using to live. What does addiction feel like? In the extreme, let the words of someone who has fallen victim do the talking.

"Several years ago, just out of college and curious to see what it was like, I accepted an injection of an opiate. My life has gone one direction since. Down. I blame no one but myself and I can live with that responsibility. But what I find increasingly impossible to live with are the losses I have brought upon myself. Not monetary or possession losses, though both have been catastrophic. But personal and emotional losses which have left me unbearably alone. I feel isolated and abandoned. My heart feels frozen. I trust no one. I long for the desire to be interested in work, in friends, in just getting out and spending money on something fun, instead of looking at everything and everyone in terms of how they might enable me to get a drug. When my parents confronted me about my use of drugs and some legal problems that have resulted, I insisted I was not physically addicted. But what I was really concealing was my psychological addiction, my love affair with the needle, a love more powerful than my love for anyone. I've lost so much—my self-respect, friends, something indefinable inside. I withdraw around people. I don't want to be touched or touch. I am dying inside." (See Suggested Reading, Pickhardt, 1983, p. 159.)

Not every case of addiction is so profoundly destructive. The severity varies from individual to individual. In all cases, however, entrapment in a self-perpetuating cycle of self-defeat is established, increasing personal suffering as it reduces power of personal choice. In moments of remorse, the person can sometimes perceive the damage being done; in moments of relapse, he or she usually cannot. Enabled by *delusion* ("It's what makes life worth living") and by *denial* ("It's not creating any problems I can't handle"), the addict cannot be reasoned or punished out of addiction by parents desperate to stop this self-inflicted damage to their child. A few points that can be helpful for parents to remember are:

51

- They did not cause the child's addiction, cannot control it, and cannot cure it.
- Making addictive choices does not mean that the child chose to become addicted.
- The child is not acting addicted to hurt the parents or the family.
- The child is not happy in addiction, creating more unhappiness day by day.
- The child does not have intentional control over the addiction, only over choosing to admit that control is lost.

Two Kinds of Addiction

Choice of substance can make a difference. Although most any substance (and activity) can become *psychologically addictive*, only some tend to become *physically addictive*. Stimulants (cocaine, for example), depressants (alcohol, for example), and narcotics (heroin, for example) are more likely to become physically addicting than inhalants (paint thinner, for example) or hallucinogens (LSD, for example). Whether marijuana can be physically addictive seems open to debate (it meets the criterion of tolerance but not withdrawal, see "physical addiction" on page 53).

Psychological addiction has to do with emotional dependence: coming to depend on the habitual, self-destructive use of a substance as a strategy for survival. The young person may come to rely on a substance to seek pleasure, to gather courage, to bolster esteem, to relieve anxiety, to lose cares, to relax tension, to flee pain, or to channel anger. The young man or woman *feels* he or she cannot manage life without depending on this substance even though using it is causing repeated personal problems. Three common signs of psychological addiction are:

1. *Compulsion* (feeling driven to use out of overpowering emotional need)

2. *Escape* (using to avoid dealing with what is painful or to cope with what feels difficult)

3. *Denial* (refusing to admit that use is causing problems)

Physical addiction has to do with physiological dependence: the person's physical system changes to adapt to repeated use of a drug. It is these changes in how the person's system functions that become the basis for physical dependence. Once this dependence is established (on caffeine, to give a mild, but common example many people can relate to), cutting back or stopping use of the drug can create withdrawal symptoms (headaches, for example). During this withdrawal period, absence of the drug often creates the opposing effects of use. Coming to depend on caffeine as a stimulant, the former user experiences fatigue upon withdrawal.

Three common signs of physical addiction are:

1. *Craving* (an overpowering physical "hunger" for the drug: "I have to have a couple cups of coffee to get started each day.")

2. *Tolerance* (increasing amounts of the drug are often required to achieve the same desired effect: "I can drink a dozen cups of coffee a day and it doesn't seem to bother me.")

3. *Withdrawal* (for an initial period of adjustment, discomforting or painful symptoms are experienced when the person's system is forced to function without the drug: "It's been two days since I stopped drinking coffee, I've got this headache that won't quit, and I feel really tired and down.")

Dependence on caffeine, although a lesser central nervous system stimulant, is an instructive addiction to look at in many ways because it illustrates a number of additional properties about addiction itself. For example, although the price for coffee has increased manyfold over the past ten to fifteen years, sales have not diminished. *To the addict, money is no object when it comes to obtaining his or her substance of choice.* Caffeine (present in coffee, tea, colas, other soft drinks, chocolate, and some over-the-counter pain relievers and wakefulness aids) is generally viewed as a harmless substance; therefore, what harm can an addiction to caffeine do? There are two kinds of harm:

1. *There is no such thing as a harmless addiction* because once an addictive pattern of behavior is in place, others, perhaps to more destructive substances, can be more easily established. Many addicts are multiply-addicted people—alcoholics who are also addicted to coffee and cigarettes, for example.

2. *One addiction can trigger other addictions.* To have coffee can become a vehicle for adding refined sugar, provide a cue for smoking a cigarette, or serve as an excuse for having a simple carbohydrate like a doughnut or something else sweet to eat, which is extremely destructive for a compulsive overeater.

Now consider signs of more serious substance addictions.

Clues of Addiction

There are numerous behaviors that tend to accompany a young person's addiction that serve as clues for which parents can watch.

- *Memory loss:* "I can't remember what I did at the party."
- *Tolerance boasts:* "I hold alcohol much better than I used to; now it takes much more to get me drunk."

- *Binge drinking:* "I don't drink all the time, but when I do I like to drink a lot." (Four drinks in a row for women or five in a row for men meets one definition of binge drinking.)

- *Denial of repeated problems:* "A couple of accidents don't have anything to do with driving a little high."

- *Withdrawal discomfort:* "I get edgy if I have to go all day at school without smoking a single cigarette."

- *Self-medication:* "I only take them to pep me up."

- *Broken promises:* "I tried to stop, and next time I will."

- *Isolating in the family:* "Just leave me alone!"

- *Tendency to blame:* "It's you and other people on my case that are causing all the problems."

- *Divided self:* "When I use, the ugly side of me comes out."

- *Secrecy and lying:* "It wasn't mine, and besides you've got no right searching my room even if it was."

- *Manipulation:* "If you want me to get a job, give me some money to get some decent clothes."

If parents even suspect addiction, the best advice is: *When in doubt, check it out.* As a family, go to a certified drug abuse counselor, facility, hospital, or treatment center to assess to what degree *substance dependence* is a disorganizing factor in the child's life and to what degree *family functioning and parenting* have become disorganized in response.

When addiction takes root in a family, the whole family needs recovery help.

10

CODEPENDENCY
WHEN PARENTS JOIN IN THE
SELF-DESTRUCTION

When severe substance problems afflict their child, parents soon find that the entire family system becomes adversely affected. Traditional parental rules, expectations, and strategies that have supported normal family life now prove insufficient to the task of coping with this unhealthy new behavior in their midst. For the first time, parents may be faced with some of the following problems:

- *Ineffectiveness:* many of their efforts to make things better create no improvement or even make things worse. For example, helping the child out of trouble only seems to help him act more irresponsibly.

- *Irresolution:* working through conflicts with their child often doesn't settle them. For example, after arguing and finally agreeing with what they want, the child then violates the agreement she has made.

- *Exploitation:* parental trust and giving are increasingly taken advantage of. For example, taking the child's word often means being taken in by lies.

- *Over- or underreactivity:* confrontation more frequently results in overreactions, whereas avoiding encounters lets serious problems go. For example, either tempers are easily lost or parents tiptoe around significant issues in order not to get the child upset.

- *Counterproductive measures:* the more controlling parents try to become, the more out of control the child often seems to get. For example, the more rules parents make, the more rules there are to get broken.

- *Costly chaos:* as order breaks down, stress begins to take a more serious toll on the parents than on the addicted child who gains freedom as traditional family structure seems to fall apart. For example, while obsessive preoccupation with what the child will or won't do next exhausts parents with anxiety, the child gathers power through increased unpredictability.

The Transition into Codependency

As family functioning becomes more disorganized, parents typically make two subtle but very significant shifts in their parenting that sets the stage for the damages to follow.

1. From having been the initiators for what needs to happen in the family, *they become primarily reactors* to what is happening, effectively ceding family influence to the substance-abusing or addicted child. (This is why part of parental recovery from codependency is reclaiming initiative to run the family.)

2. From demanding that the child live on their terms as a responsible family member, *they find themselves increasingly living on the emergent and impulsive terms set by the child.* (This is why another part of parental recovery from codependency is resetting acceptable terms for healthy family membership.)

Although this disorganization of family functioning feels confusing to parents, what is taking place is actually a lawful, albeit unhealthy, process of adjustment to cope with their child's substance-affected behavior. *The term used to describe this adjustment is Codependency.*

Codependency describes what happens to the conduct of communication, the definition of roles, and the interactions between family members when the dominant power in the family becomes the substance abuser or addict. When it is the child who has fallen victim to substances, parents increasingly *depend* their decisions, for how to feel, what to think, and what to do, on the child's self-destructive behavior. In consequence, parents experience at least three harmful effects.

1. Through preoccupation with the abusing or addicted child's problems, parents neglect and sacrifice their own well-being (and those of other children in the family) to their physical and emotional cost.

2. Through sincere but misguided efforts, parents end up supporting those problems they are trying to stop.

3. Through believing they are supposed to fix the child's behavior, parents take too much responsibility, discouraging the child from assuming responsibility enough.

Avoiding Codependent Interactions

Now the stage is set for a host of entrapping interactions between the chemically dependent child and the codependent parents that help maintain, or *enable*, the substance-related problems or make them worse. *Enabling is disabling because it increases the psychological and physical dependency it is meant to stop.* A simple way to identify some of these *codependent traps* is in the form of dialogues from which parents need to stay away.

The child says:	The parents say:
"It's all your fault!" (Blame)	"It's all our fault!" (Guilt)
"Don't let me get into trouble!" (Plead)	"We'll get you out." (Rescue)
"From now on I'll be different." (Promise)	"This time you'll change." (Hope)
"I overslept again." (Confess)	"We'll say you're sick." (Excuse)
"All I do is mess up!" (Self-pity)	"You didn't mean to." (Forgiveness)
"Give me another try." (Insistence)	"Okay, one more chance." (Exception)
"If you don't, I will." (Threat)	"If you need, we will." (Concession)
"You don't love me!" (Accuse)	"To show we do, we'll let you." (Compliance)
"It's not my fault." (Denial)	"It's not your fault." (Denial)
"You can't stop me." (Defiance)	"We can't stop you." (Helplessness)
"I swear it's the truth!" (Lying)	"We'll take your word." (Trust)
"Please don't tell!" (Concealment)	"We won't tell." (Cover up)
"Get off my case!" (Complaint)	"Not 'til you change your mind." (Control)

Complete any one of these interactions as scripted, and more often than not parents will help perpetuate (*enable*) the dependent child's problems, as well as their own problems with the child.

When a person begins to use substances in an addictive way, he or she begins to use people for freedom and resources to support that substance use. Because they care so much (want to believe the best, fear for the worst, tend to fault themselves, and want to give from love), the easiest people to exploit are usually family members. This is why for the substance-dependent child, *parents become the codependents of primary choice.* Codependency is a collusion between an exploitive child for whom substance use comes first, and enabling parents for whom saving their troubled child from herself comes first. "We'll do anything to keep her from harm. *We love her to death!*" And at its very worst, codependency can do exactly that: in service of misguided love, it can encourage the child to a self-destructive end.

This is *not* to say that parental codependency causes chemical dependence in the child. It only supports continuation of the substance problem. In most cases, however, unless and until parents extricate themselves from their enabling ways, by seeking recovery in counseling, treatment, or self-help groups like Al-Anon (see Key 31), it is very difficult for the child to let go of the chemical involvement that is ruling his or her life.

Basic Recovery from Codependency

In its own way, codependency can be every bit as debilitating as chemical dependence itself, and recovery every bit as difficult. To understand why this is so, it helps to compare the addict's dependence on the substance with the codependent's enmeshment in the addict's troubled life.

The addict is focused on self at the expense of others, preoccupied with taking care of his or her urgent chemical needs regardless of personal cost and exploiting help (most frequently from loved ones) to enable further use. In contrast, *the codependent is focused on the addicted person at the expense of self*, so preoccupied with preventing and repairing damage to the addict and to the family that he or she is at risk of abandoning adequate self-care.

The great personal danger of codependency is unhealthy self-sacrifice, doing everything possible to keep the substance abuser or addict off drugs and out of trouble, in the process coming to increasingly live on terms of *psychological, physical,* and *social self-neglect.* Because codependents are *tireless* in their efforts, they are *exhausted* most of the time.

- *Psychologically,* the codependent is at risk of ignoring his or her emotional needs—stress from unacknowledged feelings building up.

- *Physically,* the codependent is at risk of forsaking healthy bodily care—stress from inadequate rest running his or her system down.

- *Socially,* the codependent is at risk of going it alone, out of pride or shame refusing the need for external help—stress arising from anxiety at feeling isolated and unsupported.

At a minimum, to avoid codependency, or to recover from its grip, parents need to:

- Recognize hard feelings and talk them out when they arise
- Make time to adequately unwind, sleep, and renew
- Reach out for social companionship, communication, and comfort to people (like those in Al-Anon) who can relate to the trials they are going through

11

‸‸

SIGNS OF SUSCEPTIBILITY

RECEPTIVE TRAITS AND
NEGATIVE HABITUATION

Independent of genetic influence (see Key 13), parents may be able to gauge their child's susceptibility to problem involvement with substances (should use occur) by monitoring certain traits and patterns of habituation that their child exhibits.

Receptive Traits

There is some professional disagreement over the concept of an "addictive personality" (a constellation of personality traits that may predispose people to become addicted) and, if valid, over whether these traits are cause or consequence of the problem. Without entering this debate, it seems that young people who bring into counseling harmful involvement with substances often present some of the following *receptive traits*.

- *Social dependence* (are excessively reliant on peer influence and parental care-taking)

- *Excitement driven* (consider the ordinary too boring to bear)

- *Low impulse control* (find it very difficult to delay immediate gratification)

- *Tyranny of now* (can't see beyond the present)

- *Evasion of responsibility* (tend to blame others for one's own bad choices)
- *Self-deception* (lie to oneself to deny harsh reality)
- *Avoidance of the unpleasant* (keep putting off or getting around unwanted tasks)
- *Alienation from the system* (have a sense of being an outsider or a "different" individual)
- *Escape from negative emotion* (run away from the acknowledgment of painful feelings)
- *Rebellion* (actively and passively oppose external limits and demands for refusal's sake)
- *Dramatizing experience* (being drawn to exciting extremes)

Affirmative Traits

Should the receptive traits mentioned above develop (as some of them often do with the onset of adolescence), parents may want to encourage affirmative traits, which are their counterparts.

- *Self-reliance* over social dependence ("Independence means making your own decisions, as well as learning to do more for yourself instead.")
- *Appreciation of the ordinary* over being excitement driven ("Enjoying the simple, everyday parts of life can feel rewarding and relaxing.")
- *Delay of gratification* over immediate satisfaction ("Learning to wait for what you want can reduce the urgency you give to what you're waiting for.")
- *Developing future goals* over the tyranny of now ("Having something to work for can give direction to your life.")
- *Ownership of choice and consequence* over casting off responsibility ("When you blame others, you just make a victim of yourself.")

- *Honesty* over self-deception ("Pretending what isn't so won't protect you from the way things truly are.")
- *Encountering* over avoiding the unpleasant ("Deal with hard things now, and they won't hang over you later on.")
- *Social belonging* over alienation ("You can be a member of an organized group and still preserve your individuality.")
- *Cooperating with authority* over resistance ("When you work with us on what we want, we are more likely to work with you on what you want.")
- *Moderating* over dramatizing experience ("Life can be less stressful not living at the mercy of extremes.")

The Nature of Habituation

Human beings are creatures of habit. Through repeated choices, patterns of behavior are learned in the past on which people partly rely to determine how they act and react in the present. Habits are *efficient* because they allow people to simplify their lives by not having to decide everything afresh each day (how to do hygiene, how to get to school or work, or how to express feelings, for example). And habits are *supportive* because they create a predictable pattern of behavior that people can anticipate (how to start and end tomorrow, for example).

The most important thing for parents to remember about habits is that they can be good servants (when sustaining healthy functioning) but also bad masters (when inducing unhealthy functioning.) Because habits can be good or bad, parents can monitor their child's habits to encourage the good ones, and to help free the child from any that are causing harm. *The more that bad habits are in place, the less robust are the good ones, the more the child may be at risk of harmful involvement with substances when and if use begins.*

Good and Bad Habits

Categories of *good habits* can include the following.

- *Rituals*—repeat activities that promote feelings of well-being to no ill effect. For example, the child likes to start off each lunch at school with the same snack because the familiarity not only tastes good but feels good as well.

- *Routines*—recurring patterns of self-management that simplify and organize decisions made throughout each day. For example, the child reserves the two hours after supper to do homework.

- *Disciplines*—regular activities that nourish health and sustain growth. For example, the child commits to a regimen of working out to enjoy the feelings of physical well-being that result.

Categories of *bad habits* can include the following.

- *Superstitions*—magical activities supposed to ward off luck considered bad, or to court luck that is considered good. For example, maybe the child "must wear" the same pair of blue jeans every Monday if the week is to get off to a promising start.

- *Compulsions*—driven activities to control fears that only make fear worse. For example, to feel safe, the child "has to" get up multiple times each night to make sure all the doors in the house are locked.

- *Addictions*—self-destructive activities upon which a person comes to depend for survival. For example, the child "can't help" binge eating to satisfy some psychological hunger and then purging to compensate for the damage done.

Reducing Susceptibility

To reduce a child's susceptibility to problem involvement with substances, parents can:

1. Encourage development of affirmative traits that are opposite to those receptive traits commonly associated with problem use

2. Support the development of constructive habits that enhance healthy functioning

3. Get counseling for their child to help overcome the destructive harm that compulsions and nonsubstance addictions can do

12

PARENTAL USE

**WHAT CHILDREN SEE IS WHAT
THEY LEARN**

The best preventive (although no guarantee) for ensuring drug-free children is having drug-free parents. Why? Because parents can have a powerful influence on children's inclination to substance use in at least five ways.

1. *The ingredients of family functioning* have formative effect, because it is these ordinary components that teach children what constitutes the "normal" conduct of family life. Thus, it can make a difference if parental use of substances is nonexistent or occasional (no major contributor to family functioning), or if it appears essential (there is a daily "cocktail hour," for example), causing parents to schedule regular use into their life as a sign of its importance and showing signs of missing it when they do not.

2. *The self-medication by parents* has formative effect, because children learn to follow a lot of the examples parents set. Thus, it can make a difference if parents only model drug use for the relief of physical or emotional discomfort based on a physician's prescription, or if they self-prescribe a variety of over-the-counter, natural remedy, and recreational substances to relax, reduce emotional distress, promote wellness, prevent problems, or increase sense of well-being on their own authority.

3. *The attitude parents express* has formative effect, because children learn to evaluate the world through the lens of their parents' values. Thus, it can make a difference if parents express attitudes that disapprove the entertaining images of excessive substance use presented through the popular media, or if they condone presentations of getting drunk, stoned, high, or wasted as an acceptable, fun, or funny thing to do.

4. *The communication parents give* has a formative effect, because in what they are willing and not willing to talk about, they declare to children which subjects are open for discussion and which are not. Thus, it can make a difference if parents matter-of-factly answer questions and initiate conversation about their own substance use, or if they censure such discussions in an effort to defend or conceal what is going on.

5. *The way parents socialize* has formative effect, because it demonstrates how good times with friends are to be had. Thus, it can make a difference if parents often have company over and extend hospitality without offering drugs or alcohol, or if chemicals are socially required to make the occasion relaxing, convivial, or fun.

The model is the message. "Children whose parents smoke are more than twice as likely to use cigarettes eventually than are the children of nonsmokers. In the same way, if either parent is a heavy alcohol or drug user, a child is much more likely to become involved in their use, due to both exposure and availability." (See Suggested Reading, Schor, p. 54.)

Drug-free Parents

What are drug-free parents? Here are *five criteria*:

- Drug-free parents are free from any drive to use. Should they use, they do so out of recreational want, not out of any compelling regular need, because doing without is as comfortable and free of problems as deciding to use.

- Drug-free parents freely resort to other activities for relaxing tension, reducing emotional discomfort, or increasing well-being besides relying on substance use.

- Drug-free parents freely editorialize to their children about responsible and irresponsible examples of substance use as presented in the popular media and enacted in their world of experience.

- Drug-free parents freely discuss their own substance use with their children without defense, distortion, or denial.

- Drug-free parents freely entertain friends without always requiring substance use to be part of the fun. When they use, they do so in moderation.

It is worth mentioning that when parents themselves are substance addicted, they are distinctly *not* drug-free. Not only are they usually unable to meet the five criteria described above, but should their child abuse or become dependent on substances, they can become extremely destructive enablers. To protect their overpowering dependence, they may deny their child's use because to recognize that problem is to risk discovery of their own. The question they face can be an excruciating one: Which matters more, their reliance on drugs or their love for their child?

Parental Use and the Prohibition of Child Use

"Well you do it, so why shouldn't I?" argues the adolescent, angry that he or she should be subject to rules that the rule makers—the parents—can live above with impunity.

Sometimes parents feel hard-pressed to make a reasonable response to this challenge of their authority.

Just because they may choose to drink or smoke or use other recreational substances, doesn't mean that parents should not prohibit these behaviors to their child. After all, a host of double standards about freedom separate being considered an adult and being a child. For dangerous freedoms (like driving a car, having sex, drinking alcohol, for example) to be relatively safe, the self-protection of adequate knowledge, restraint, and responsibility is required. It takes years of growing up to develop these protective traits, and the child still has years to go.

Nonetheless, it is also true that substance-using parents are more likely to have substance-using children. Parental models are very hard to resist. If parents, however, are regretfully dependent on a substance (like dipping or smoking tobacco, for example) and want their child to follow their advice and not their example, they can describe:

- Their history with the substance
- Their efforts to quit over the years
- The health, performance, and relationship problems that have been created
- The financial costs involved
- How it feels to be victim of an overpowering habit they cannot manage to give up

Quitting and recovering are powerful examples to give a child, but if parents can do neither, they can remind the child: *Every parent gives a child not one model to follow, but two—how to be, and how not to be.* For the nicotine-dependent parent who wishes he or she could kick the habit but cannot, a forthright admission of this negative example can often have a positive instructional effect.

13

‸‸

FAMILY HISTORY
PATTERNS CAN REPEAT DOWN
THE GENERATIONS

The transmission of a heightened susceptibility to substances from one generation to the next should be an active concern of parents who have chemical dependency, or other forms of addictive behavior, in their family history.

"Blood relatives of alcoholics have a higher incidence of alcoholism than people at random." (See Suggested Reading, Merck, p. 443.) What many experts believe is that addiction to alcohol in particular, and perhaps addiction in general (see Suggested Reading, Phelps and Nourse, p. 22) may be transmitted through some kind of inherited genetic susceptibility.

Owning Family History

This finding suggests that even if parents are relatively drug-free or entirely abstinent, existence of chemical dependency among their siblings or parents, for example, can still place their child in a higher category of risk for problem involvement should substance use occur. This is not a matter of certainty (the child preordained to become addicted) but of probability (the statistical likelihood of addiction is increased).

Given this inherited vulnerability, what can parents do to protect their child? *Inform* the boy or girl about this danger so he or she is given cause to proceed extremely carefully should the decision to use ever be made. Describe to the child who in the biologically extended family system, in the last three generations, has been, or is, chemically or otherwise addicted.

"But we can't do that!" argue some parents. "If our child found out that her grandmother is addicted to tranquilizers and that her grandfather is a closet alcoholic, she'd lose respect for them. They'd be furious at us for telling what we've always been expected to conceal and they still deny. You don't understand. It's supposed to be kept secret!"

There are two problems with family secrets. First, they are rarely kept as secret as the controlling, fearful, guilty, or ashamed person likes to think. Most family secrets are really well known but agreed upon lies. And second, as long as the intent of secrecy prevails, a serious problem goes unattended, vital knowledge is withheld, and ignorance or denial rule.

Because addiction is so often cloaked in secrecy enforced by threat or shame, it is often excluded from accounts of family past. Like suicide, it is frequently omitted from the history that parents have been told in order to preserve that family's, or that family member's, reputation. For this reason, many parents do not know what they need to know. Therefore, exploring with adult siblings and older relatives the possibility of substance abuse or addiction in one's family background can sometimes be enlightening.

A healthy family has an open communication system in which problems are freely recognized and frankly discussed. Parents need to ask themselves: if any other genetically transmitted disease were in the child's immediate family history, would they want their child to know so risk awareness could be gained and precautions taken? For example, if a history of hemophilia or cystic fibrosis existed, would parents want their child to know? If so, then treat addiction in the family just the same.

In addition to learning about his or her possible inherited predisposition to addiction, the boy or girl can become additionally mindful about substance use when parents describe what they know about the afflicted family member's experience with addiction—when and how it may have started, troubles it may have caused over the years, how others may have been affected, and how recovery was gained, if it was. *There is always a cautionary tale to be told*, a specific family example the child can keep in mind as a familiar reference for the harm that substances can do.

Identifying Family Patterns

The likelihood of addiction being transmitted to or through one family generation to the next may not simply be a matter of genetics. There is also the influence of social learning to be considered.

Addiction and codependency are linked sets of behaviors. Each can be encouraged to provide a complement to the other, with the relationship between the two shaping how people learn to interact with each other in a family. For example, as an addicted family member becomes more self-indulgent, impulsive, out of control, inconsiderate, and blaming, other family members can compensate by acting codependently. They can become more self-sacrificial, constrained, controlling, oversensitive, and guilty for problems that are going on and strive to make up in the family for responsible conduct they feel the addicted person lacks. "I learned to take the bullet for my brother to save our family from embarrassment when he went off on one of his frequent tears."

To a significant degree, people are shaped in their families of origin, learning to occupy a large number of the social and psychological roles they will live in for the rest of their lives. Families are formative. They teach children how to treat themselves, how to treat others, and how they should be treated in return. Unhappily, when parents, in growing up, learn codependent roles (to survive with an addicted parent, for example), they are inclined to reenact those roles as adults. This follows in families of their own when faced with a child whose behavior is painfully reminiscent of what they once knew.

Thus, when their teenager starts the pushing against, getting around, falling away, and acting out behaviors so often associated with early substance abuse, instead of enforcing a healthy set of demands and limits to restrain the situation, these parents often tend to react in old familiar codependent ways. Schooled in their family of origin to accept the unacceptable, to adjust to what is unhealthy, to look the other way, to suppress painful emotion, to withhold honest communication, to keep secrets, to blame themselves, to avoid confrontation, and to excuse irresponsible acts, they only enable their child's problems with substances.

If parents have any reason to suspect that patterns of addiction or codependency had shaping influence on their growing up, *they need to identify and own those effects*. Not to do so, particularly if they have a child who is abusing substances, will only cause them to react in ignorance of their own complicity as the situation grows from bad to worse. Gaining general knowledge helps. (See Suggested Reading, Woititz, *Adult Children Of Alcoholics*, and Beattie, *Co-Dependent No More*.)

14

~~~~~~

POPULAR CULTURE

THE MEDIA IS INSTRUCTIVE

At some point in their child's growing up, usually by the onset of adolescence (between the ages of nine and thirteen), parents have begun to experience a frightening loss of family control to a social influence apparently more powerful than their own: the popular culture and its faithful servant, the media.

"The music, the movies, the computer, the Internet, the radio, the TV, the magazines, even the newspapers, all of them! Putting ideas into our child's head we don't want her to think about. Causing her to try to grow up faster than she should. Telling her what to value and how to believe, when we don't value or believe those things. Encouraging all kinds of dangers—rebellion, sex, drugs, breaking the law, even violence. It's crazy. We end up having to fight our child to protect her from the society she's growing up in. How could we create a culture that sets our kids up for so much trouble?" How, indeed.

The experience of adolescence has a lot to do with managing the awkwardness of being "in between." No longer willing to be treated as a child, but not yet ready to be treated as an adult, the young person struggles for another definition, spending a lot of time figuring out just who and how to be by experimenting with a host of different images, experiences, beliefs, and relationships. Because of this developmental loss of identity that goes with leaving childhood for the sake of growing up, *adolescence is an extremely impressionable age.*

Searching for an alternative definition independent of family and distinct from childhood, the young person increasingly turns to the popular culture for example and instruction. The influence of this exposure can be profound.

Primarily through *entertainment* and *advertising*, the onslaught of media has formative effect. The truth about what really matters, the latest fashions that are "in," the heroes currently worshipped, the ideals promoted, the fantasies encouraged, the glamorous products sold, the compelling stories told, and the lyrics persuasively sung all prove too much for teenagers to entirely resist.

These messages teach lessons that often may *indirectly* and *directly* encourage a young person's involvement with substances.

Indirect Encouragement for Substance Use

Among the many values to live by that are promoted by popular entertainment and advertising are three of particular concern:

1. Escape from, instead of involvement with, the demands of reality

2. The sensational side of reality instead of the ordinary one

3. The quick fix for real problems instead of a slow solution

Searching for escape, sensation, and a quick fix are three prime motivations that also drive young people toward substance use.

Escape

In this country, adolescents grow up in a world where fantasy-based entertainment and electronic diversions preoccupy an ever-increasing amount of their time, encouraging them to spend untold hours each week getting away from their cares and avoiding responsibilities that parents wish they would address. Thus, parents might want to ask themselves: "How many hours a week does our child spend escaping from the challenges of life rather than in learning how to meet them?"

The Sensational

Adolescents in this country grow up in a media world of entertainment and advertising that both exploit the extremes of human experience to attract attention and create the impression that if it's not exciting, it's not worth responding to. Thus, parents might want to ask themselves: "To what degree does our child behave as though sensational experiences matter most, and anything ordinary in life is not worthwhile?"

The Quick Fix

Adolescents are constantly being fed advertising that stresses how immediate relief, rewards, or results are available to overcome most human problems and satisfy most human needs. As Leite and Parrish (see Suggested Reading) note: "There are no commercials suggesting the use of problem solving, self-discipline, or social support as a solution to pain." (page 37) Thus, parents might want to ask themselves: "To what degree does our child give up too easily on a problem because he or she lacks the determination to work a slow solution through?"

Rather than abandon their child to those seductive motivations conveyed by the popular media that can also serve to encourage substance use, parents can assert counterinfluences of their own.

- "Involvement is more important than escape from reality; you grow by facing challenges, not by running away."

- "Meeting ordinary day-to-day demands is most of what life is about; and the willingness to make them a high priority will get you further than only attending that which is exciting, sensational, fantastic, or extreme."

- "Significant problems demand patience and determination to solve; in most cases, quick fixes are temporary at best, and at worst, they don't really work at all."

Then there is the need to counter the direct influences for use.

Direct Encouragement for Substance Use

The world of popular entertainment is where most adolescent heroes live. The teenage spectator thinks: "To become like my hero, I should do as my hero does." Through imitation, young people strive for similarity to their ideals. Advertising commercially exploits this identification through using star and celebrity endorsements to influence consumer choices that children make.

Advertising also uses nameless models to powerful effect. Beautiful, handsome, sexy, and successful-looking individuals appearing confident, feeling happy, having fun, and being popular show impressionable adolescents how to live the "good" life.

Even though cigarette and alcohol advertising is not supposed to be directed at adolescents, it actually is. Using young adults as models only increases the allure of this substance use because teenagers want to identify with people more grown up.

Advertising legal drugs is successful in creating brand awareness, increasing consumer sales, and encouraging lifestyle substance use. Enormous amounts of promotional money are poured into the media, with thousands of alcohol-related ads shown on television each year. The vulnerability of children to advertising of this particular recreational substance has provoked strong medical opposition. "Alcohol is the drug most often abused by the largest number of children and adolescents. The American Academy of Pediatrics supports a ban on alcohol advertising." (See Suggested Reading, Schor, p. 54.)

Because no such ban is in place, it is up to parents to do some counteradvertising of their own. If they do not, they will abandon their child to the persuasion of promoters, whose only interest is the market potential and discretionary spending power that their child represents. Therefore, if parents see their child positively responding to substance use as portrayed through entertainment or offered through advertising, they can choose to weigh in with a second opinion of their own. If the child thinks that the image or example of substance use is "cool," parents can say why they do not.

How they disagree, however, is critical to the success of their message—whether it is tuned out or taken in. *Controlling* the child's thinking and criticizing the child's taste is not productive because to do either only makes the child more defensive and less receptive. Instead, parents need to come from a position of honest caring and open communication, motivated by the desire to expand what the child may be willing to consider by offering a different evaluation, explanation, or perspective of their own. "We are not demanding that you change your mind, we are only asking that you listen to our point of view."

15

PEERS

FITTING IN MEANS FOLLOWING ALONG

In childhood, a boy or girl's peer group tends to be arranged by adults getting kids together for play or other recreational purposes. Come adolescence, however, in pursuit of independence, young people begin to socially organize on their own.

From this point on, parents find themselves increasingly cast to the social periphery of their child's life, as being with friends becomes a major focus of the growing boy or girl's concern. "Peers are more important than parents" is the message the adolescent seems to be sending—spending endless time and conversation on friends and having less and less of both available for family. Feeling on the losing end of this competition, some parents will complain: "We don't matter anymore!" Nothing could be farther from the truth.

Parents Are Still Primary

Despite actions and appearances to the contrary, parents matter more than ever. They provide a solid home base from which the teenager can pull away and venture forth in confidence based on having a secure and supportive place to return. Ironically, what parents take as an affront is actually a compliment. "You go to no end of trouble for your friends," they protest, "but us you just take for granted." Exactly. Although friendships come and go and can be fickle, family isn't going to disappear and parental love is here to stay.

More to the point, parental modeling is more powerful than influence from peers. During the early years of childhood, before peer groups came on the scene, parents helped shape the child's fundamental ethical beliefs and personal character. Even "the influence of bad companions is generally not able to change the character formed at home." (See Suggested Reading, Schaeffer and Millman, p. 258.)

It is when parents, perhaps insecure in relation to their emerging adolescent, act like they are often treated (feeling neglected, they neglect in response) that they deliver their child to the influence they fear: *peer pressure.* The more excluded at home, the more abandoned by parents, the more alienated from family the teenager feels, the more vulnerable to impulsive and immature decision making of "the group" he or she becomes. This vulnerability is particularly apparent around involvement with substances. *Most drug and alcohol experimentation, use, abuse, and addiction by young people is conducted in the company of like-minded friends.*

The High Costs of Social Belonging

Succumbing to peer pressure is an expression of social insecurity, of giving in to get along. The child sacrifices some degree of personal freedom in a variety of ways.

- Some *independence* will be sacrificed for the sake of conformity. ("I did it because that's what everybody else wanted to do.")

- Some *authenticity* will be sacrificed for the sake of acceptance. ("I just shut up because I didn't want to turn the others against me.")

- Some *honesty* will be sacrificed for the sake of pretense. ("I said I wanted to when I really didn't.")

- Some *individuality* will be sacrificed for the sake of group identity. ("It's what everybody has to do to be a member of the gang.")

By comparison to family, membership in peer groups can be pretty expensive. Consider just a few of the common costs for social belonging that a young person may often pay. Spoken or implied, this is the message the child receives: "To be one of us, you must appear like us, you must like what we like, you must dislike who we dislike, you must believe like us, you must behave like us, you must like us best, and you mustn't do better than us." Within the context of this social pressure, parents can well appreciate one insecure teenager's definition of what it means to *make friends*. "Making friends means making yourself into the kind of person friends will like."

What to Say When You Can't Say "No"

Appreciating the power of peer pressure, particularly pressure to use substances, that a young person can face, parents can support the strength to say "No" by complimenting the child when he or she describes acts of independence, authenticity, honesty, and individuality with friends. "Good for you! Saying 'No' is an act of self-respect and earns you respect from others."

Although this may sound contradictory, parents can also support the child's capacity to speak up and sometimes say "No" to them, even though they may not enjoy the argument and opposition. Think about it this way. Parents who treat speaking up as talking back, disagreement as disrespect, and resistance as defiance may be enforcing social obedience to the child's later social cost. *Extremely compliant children who cannot say "No" to parents are often ill prepared to say "No" to friends.*

So, consider the fourteen-year-old, hanging out after school with a group of friends, in some unsupervised place, being expected to share a joint (marijuana) or finish a bottle (alcohol) or huff a popper (amyl nitrite), afraid to say "No" because to do so might provoke criticism, conflict, or rejection. "You too good for us? You don't like what we're doing? You don't want to hang out with us anymore? You going to rat on us?" Saying "No" to substance use can feel like saying "No" to friendship itself. This is why parents need to give their child some alternatives to direct refusal when he or she feels unable or unwilling to directly say "No."

- *Play for delay.* What adolescents naturally say to turn down parental requests they can also use with peers: "Not now, later." Then, if peers increase the immediate pressure, the teenager can get angry over an issue that those exerting the pressure can respect. "Cut it out! I don't like being pushed around. Not by you or anyone! I'll do it when I feel like it, and not before!"

- *Make a temporary exit.* There are seven little words that have saved many an adolescent from becoming trapped by the momentary pressure of impulsive friends: "I need to use the rest room." Using this pretext takes the young person out of the immediate social context to a quiet, private place where he or she can think clearly about what is best to do or say to get out of this unwanted situation. Very often, upon returning to the group, the young person discovers that the previous impulse has fallen out of favor and the focus of activity has shifted to something else.

- *Make an excuse.* Not wanting to give into substance use that friends are pushing, but fearful of the social consequences of saying "No," the young person makes one of the following excuses. "I don't feel well." "I tried that before and I had a bad trip." "If I don't get home right away, I'll be grounded." "My parents drug test me, and if I show up positive they yank my car." As it happens, all four statements are lies, but they may provide the young person a convincing way out when truth feels too hard to say. Although parents would rather that the child be able to give an honest refusal, a dishonest one is better than none at all.

"Not right now," "I'll be right back," "I can't because . . .," are all part of the indirect repertoire of refusal to peer pressure that every adolescent needs.

16

FEELING "DEPRESSED"
AND DEPRESSION

DON'T MIX SUBSTANCE ABUSE
AND DESPONDENCY

The relationship between feelings of depression and drug abuse is a two-way street. Feelings of depression can cause a young person to seek escape or relief through drugs. And drug abuse (particularly with depressants) can intensify feelings of depression to self-destructive effect.

Clarifying Definitions

Before beginning this discussion, it is important to get three definitions clear.

1. *Depressed*, as it is commonly, *not* clinically, used (as in: "I feel depressed"), refers to a normal, very sad emotional experience a person can go through typically in response to acute stress, painful adversity, or significant loss. Just because a child says he or she is "feeling depressed," this declaration (*which should put parents on watch for their child*) does not mean the boy or girl is necessarily experiencing or heading for depression, particularly if he or she shows signs of positive resolve and constructive coping with the pain.

2. *Depression*, as it is clinically used (*which should cause parents to seek help for their child*), refers to a severe state of despondency in which a person becomes emotionally stuck, typically feeling trapped in hurt, hopelessness, helplessness, anger, and worthlessness, without having the energy or motivation available to make any positive change.

3. *Depressant* refers to a group of *potentially addicting drugs* (like alcohol) that "depress" or sedate symptoms of gloominess, nervousness, agitation, or insomnia, helping a person feel more calm, normal, relaxed, or able to sleep.

Putting Parents on Notice

During the inevitable ups and downs of adolescent growth (see Keys 19 to 23), times of significant, persistent sadness in their child should be taken seriously by parents because these may either be a precursor or consequence of substance abuse. What can a parent watch out for? A few common signs of feeling seriously depressed include:

- withdrawal from friends
- isolation and diminished communication within the family
- through words and tears, expressing significant unhappiness
- no longer liking, even giving up, activities previously enjoyed
- acting more angry, provoking more conflict in the family
- making statements reflecting low self-esteem
- having difficulty sleeping
- experiencing a loss of traditional appetite
- showing a drop in school achievement
- having an unusual weight loss (too thin) or weight gain (too heavy)

- expressing chronic fatigue
- becoming increasingly pessimistic about life

If a child appears unable or unwilling to talk about and work his or her way out of depressed feelings after a couple of weeks, *if* a child seems to be getting more despondent, or *if* a child accidentally or intentionally begins to do damage to himself or herself, *parents need to get the child evaluated for depression.* The best prevention from resorting to harmful self-medication or from *acting out* depressed feelings in destructive ways is getting the child into counseling where he or she can *talk out* whatever unhappiness is going on.

The Depression/Substance Abuse/Suicide Connection

Read the following quotations from reliable authorities, and the destructive interaction of depression and substance abuse comes clear.

"A child is at increased risk of suicide if . . . the child has substance abuse problems . . . Alcohol increases the risk of suicidal behavior by worsening feelings of depression and by diminishing self-control. About half of those who attempt suicide are intoxicated at the time of the attempt . . . Drug overdose is the method most frequently used in suicide attempts." (See Suggested Reading, Merck, pp. 413–414.)

"One in four youngsters will experience a serious episode of depression by the time they reach their eighteenth birthday . . . The majority of children who try to kill themselves are seriously depressed . . . The rate of suicide among teens has more than doubled over the past thirty years, making suicide the second leading cause of death among children ages fifteen to nineteen." (See Suggested Reading, Fassler and Dumas, pp. 2–3.)

"Because ninety percent of the people in the United States drink at some time during their lives, and perhaps half of drinkers have some temporary alcohol-related difficulties, problems with depressants are the most common of the substance abuse difficulties in the Western world." (See Suggested Reading, Schuckit, p. 34.)

Depressant drugs, like alcohol, are often chosen by young people as a means to relieve feeling depressed, or to escape from depression. But this substance only increases the possibility of suicidal behavior when they are suffering from this despondent experience or this despondent state.

In addition, coming down off certain stimulant or narcotic drugs can cause feelings of depression, as can withdrawal from substances to which one has become addicted. Even the struggle to give up long-term cigarette use, for example, can be extremely painful. It is the severity of this depression from quitting substance dependence that creates *the high risk of relapse in early recovery*, a risk that medical treatment, psychological counseling, and social support can all moderate. Thus, to help maintain early sobriety, Alcoholics Anonymous often recommends "ninety meetings in ninety days."

When Suicide Has Been Threatened

"The notion that a person who threatens suicide will not carry out the threat is fallacious. The communication of suicidal intent is the best single predictor of a successful suicidal attempt. Previously unsuccessful suicidal attempts are followed by successful suicides in a substantial proportion of cases." (See Suggested Reading, Beck, p. 59.)

"Even if a child is at high risk for suicide, she cannot kill herself without two things: *available method* . . . and *opportunity*, that is, the privacy to attempt suicide. This is why suicidal children need to be under extremely close watch twenty-four hours a day." (See Suggested Reading, Fassler and Dumas, p. 111.)

There are degrees of suicidal statements for parents to listen for:

1. "Sometimes I feel like life isn't worth living."

2. "I wish I were dead."

3. "I think about killing myself a lot."

4. "Cutting myself makes other pain go away."

5. "It would be so easy—just get blind drunk and drive the car off the road."

Although all five statements should be taken seriously, the level of intention and planning in levels 3, 4, and 5 warrant an immediate evaluation for a highly supervised time-out at home or protective hospitalization.

Parents can speak to their child as follows: "If you are so unhappy that suicide seems to be your best choice for dealing with the pain, then we need to get you help to find other choices that will improve your life, not end it. We will act to make sure that

• you will get to talk out your unhappiness with someone who understands how you feel.

• you will be adequately supervised for your protection.

• you will be kept free of any recreational substance use, and your past use will be evaluated.

• you will not have ready means for self-destruction available to you as long as you are at risk of this unhappy and impulsive state."

In line with this last commitment, parents either remove or secure any common suicidal means on the household premises, including prescription and over-the-counter medications, household poisons, knives and razor blades, rope, guns and other weapons, and access to any motor vehicles.

One of the most common scenarios leading to suicide plays out as follows.

1. Getting into a depressed state from a performance failure or relationship loss. (Therefore, take significant failures or losses seriously and hear hurt feelings out.)

2. Withdrawing into psychological or social isolation to conceal lowered self-esteem. (Therefore, increase support and expressions of personal affirmation.)

3. Allowing distorted thinking to create an exaggerated picture of hopelessness and helplessness. (Therefore, provide a realistic perspective.)

4. Resorting to substance use to self-medicate pain, thereby increasing the likelihood that impulse may rule. (Therefore, discourage resort to drugs and alcohol, and encourage deliberately talking the suffering through.)

5. Having access to a ready means to end suffering by ending life. (Therefore, secure all household means for inflicting serious self-harm.)

The old adage truly applies: "It's better to be safe than sorry." *Therefore, always evaluate the possible link between substance abuse and depression, because the connection can be suicidal.*

17

BOREDOM

A DANGEROUS STATE OF MIND

"Kid stuff is *boring!*" "Stop treating me like a child!" "I'm too old to do that anymore!"

Somewhere between the ages of nine and thirteen, a boy or girl usually declares independence from childhood. For adolescent growth to begin, the traditional boundaries that defined and confined the child must to a degree be broken in order to create freedom to grow. In words and actions, the adolescent rejects the old identity for the new, by communicating:

- "I am different from how I was as a child."
- "I am going to be different from how you are as my parents."
- "I am going to be different from how you want me to be."

These statements of rejection all inform parents that the age of childhood has ended and the separation into adolescence has begun.

Boredom as an Expression of Developmental Loss

In an effort to differentiate from the child he or she was, the adolescent may throw away some childish things—interests (sports), activities (scouts), relationships (old friends), image (traditional dress), and role (family helper). Although these old parts of self meant a lot as a child, to retain them all would mean that he or she was still acting like a child. Now, two problems are created. First, these losses can be missed, so there is *grief*: "Sometimes I wish I could go back to the way I was." And second, there is nothing yet to replace what has been given up, so there is *boredom*: "I don't know what to do with myself!" But when concerned parents offer helpful suggestions, the boy or girl turns them down because one credential for becoming an adolescent is no longer fitting in or being truly understood by family: "You don't know what's best for me! You just don't understand!"

It's tempting for parents to discount and dismiss youthful boredom as a normal part of adolescent growth. Just because it's normal, however, doesn't mean that it should be ignored. Many parents underestimate the powerful role of boredom as a motivation in their adolescent child and fail to appreciate the risks, *particularly risks of substance involvement*, that this disaffected and aimless state can pose. *Boredom is a staging area from which a lot of adolescent recklessness begins, particularly resorting to alcohol and drugs.*

Suffering from Boredom Can Encourage Escape from Pain

Boredom is a hard human experience to define precisely because, like its cousin depression, it is complex and multiply determined. Boredom and depression both have at their core a sense of deficiency. In depression, the person lacks esteem and feels worthless. In boredom, the person lacks internal resources and feels that there is nothing worth doing. At worst, expressions of boredom can be precursors to, or signs of, depression.

When the teenager complains: "Boredom is a *pain*, I hate it!" he or she isn't lying. Although many parents tend to trivialize boredom or respond impatiently to its expression, the truth is that boredom can significantly hurt the adolescent in at least three ways.

1. *Loneliness* from boredom is commonly expressed as a lack of feeling connected: "I'm at loose ends." This usually means that the adolescent has no good feeling way to companion himself or herself, or to enjoy the companionship of friends.

2. *Emptiness* from boredom is commonly expressed as a lack of self-sufficiency: "There's nothing I can do with myself." This usually means that the adolescent has looked inside himself or herself only to discover no satisfying sense of purpose there.

3. *Dullness* from boredom is commonly expressed as a lack of stimulation: "There's nothing fun to do!" This usually means that the adolescent is dissatisfied and restless, finding daily experience unbearably dreary and unrewarding.

The danger of boredom is in the temptations it creates—for escape to relieve the pain.

- Loneliness creates the *temptation to succumb to the influence of impulsive peers,* because doing anything with someone feels preferable to doing nothing alone. "After laying around and not finding anyone all weekend, I was ready to party if that's what my friends wanted to do."

- Emptiness creates the *temptation to experiment with new experience* to fill up the inner void. "I couldn't stand feeling nothing inside, so I dropped some acid and it gave me a sense of myself I'd never had before."

- Dullness creates the *temptation to seek excitement from stimulation.* "When I first heard about cocaine, I knew that kind of rush was made for me—a high that felt like it had no top."

Antidotes to Boredom

Knowing some of the major temptations that boredom can offer, parents can counter these risks by supporting *antidote activities*.

- Loneliness is countered by *involvement in relationships* (joining a church youth group, for example).

- Emptiness is countered by *pursuing interests* (learning to play a musical instrument, for example).

- Dullness is countered by *undertaking a challenge* (testing one's limits through competition in sports, for example).

Although intermittent experiences of boredom are to be expected during adolescence, and although constructively coping with this sense of aimlessness is an important responsibility to learn, days of a child feeling bored, like days of feeling depressed, warrant parental attention and intervention.

The Importance of Goals

The most powerful antidotes to boredom are goals. Goal-directed children are engaged on their own behalf in activities that matter to them, and hopefully to their parents as well. When their adolescent is truly at a protracted loss of knowing what to do with himself or herself, suffering from the pain of boredom, parents should initiate an exploration of meaningful possibilities.

This exploration may be done by opening up a world of choices through which the adolescent can identify a purpose or a process that might yield a meaningful result. Parents might initiate this discussion: "Boredom means it's time to make a change because you are dissatisfied with how you feel. So, let's talk about possible activities you could begin. We want you to do something, but what exactly is mostly up to you. For example, you could create, join, play, learn, earn, accomplish, achieve, plan, discuss, read, compete, help, volunteer, apprentice, work, study, practice, or investigate to produce an experience or outcome you would enjoy."

Although adolescents can be stubbornly resistant ("There's no point, there's nothing I want to do, leave me alone!"), parents need to keep pushing their agenda for meaningful engagement. *Protracted boredom is no safe place for an adolescent to stay, both because of its potential as a staging area for drug use and as a possible precursor or symptom of depression.*

18

‸‸

SELF-ESTEEM

THE DANGER WHEN
SELF-WORTH RUNS LOW

D oes a young person ever abuse drugs or alcohol in order to escape or medicate suffering from low self-esteem, or does self-esteem ever become lowered as a result of abusing drugs or alcohol? The answer to both parts of this question is "Yes." Substance abuse and addiction can be both the cause and consequence of low self-esteem. Therefore: Key to the prevention of, and recovery from, substance abuse and addiction is helping the child build and maintain a strong, positive sense of self-esteem.

What Is Self-esteem?

But what precisely is self-esteem? Because it is a very popular and very vague psychological concept, parents will find it hard to specifically encourage its growth unless they can give self-esteem a specific description.

Begin with the following definition. *Self-esteem is a* self-evaluation *made according to certain subjective* criteria *that a person believes are* relevant *for determining his or her human* worth.

Self-esteem is *not* a constant. It can fluctuate between positive and negative based on physical state (well or ill), life experience (succeed or fail), and mood (happy or sad). Over time, most people go through ups and downs in self-esteem, including some periods when they feel good about themselves and other periods when they do not.

Thus, if a boy or girl is going through a passage of low self-esteem, that doesn't mean something is wrong with the child. There is now a challenge to recover a better self-evaluation by altering behavior (doing better in school, for example) or by changing personal standards (judging himself or herself less harshly, for example). What is *wrong* is to act in ways that lower self-esteem, or to deal with low self-esteem in ways that only drive it further down. *Resorting to substances is a wrong choice because the short-term payoff of feeling better is usually followed by the longer-term consequence of making the problem worse.*

Consider the following dialogue as an example.

Client: "I felt shy. A real social failure. I hated it. Everyone else had a good time at parties. They could talk and laugh and enjoy fooling around. Not me. I just sat on the sidelines. I couldn't say a word. I was frozen shut. But not anymore! I drink before the party. I've got a buzz on when I get there. Now I'm not afraid of speaking up. And I'm free to act crazy like everybody else!"

Psychologist: "So drinking has helped make you not shy anymore?"

Client: "No. I didn't say that. I'm probably more shy now than I was before. I just don't deal with it. I just drink enough so it doesn't matter."

In this young person's case, being a social success was important for self-esteem. Failing to measure up to that criterion caused suffering. Resorting to alcohol for pain relief and liquid courage only substituted a substance problem for a problem with social shyness, with the latter getting worse through avoidance and neglect.

Criteria for Measuring Self-esteem
Many and varied are the criteria by which people mea-

sure their self-esteem. What is an essential criterion for one person (orderly surroundings for an adult who likes be in control and neat, for example) can be opposite to another (a messy room for a teenager who likes freedom to be disorganized, for example).

Between boys and girls, however, there are some differences between how male and female still tend to be socialized around self-esteem to which parents can be sensitive. For young women, the criteria for self-esteem often have a *relational* focus—to feel good about themselves, being connected to close and confiding friends may be most important. For young men, the criteria for self-esteem often have a *performance* focus—to feel good about themselves, competing or achieving well may be most important. Thus, having a good friend move away may pose more threat to a young woman's self-esteem than a young man's, whereas losing a starting position on the team may pose more threat to a young man's self-esteem than to a young woman's.

The main point for parents is to understand your child well enough to know when hard life experience has caused a significant criterion of self-esteem to go unmet. And to be willing to *engage* with the child at this point to forestall the likelihood that the boy or girl will seek a chemical fix for his or her diminished sense of worth. Engage how? By helping the child talk out what happened. Encourage the child to share his or her feelings. Listening (not correcting) is the key, so the boy or girl receives parental support when life delivers such an unwelcome blow.

Attitude, Beliefs, and Treatment—Three Important Pillars of Self-esteem

Thus, parents sympathize and comfort the child whose romantic attachment has just broken up, that relationship having been a major source of self-esteem for over a year.

They also listen and observe carefully to monitor three supports on which the child depends for self-esteem, and which the child *chooses* to construct in positive or negative terms.

1. *Attitude:* How does the child *feel* about himself or herself, about other people, and about life, in consequence of this important loss?

2. *Beliefs:* What does the child *think* about himself or herself in light of the recent hurt?

3. *Treatment:* How does the child *act* toward himself or others in consequence of what has occurred?

If the child says: "I hate myself!" "I'll never trust again!" "Life never works out the way I want!" parents need to speak up. Rather than let these negative *attitudes* go unchallenged and reduce self-esteem even further, they need to offer affirmative alternatives: "It's love, and trust, and optimism that keep a person feeling worthwhile and that life is worth living. Your attitude has a lot to do with how your experiences will be."

If the child says: "There's something wrong with me," "Nobody could really love someone like me," then parents need to speak up. Rather than let these negative *beliefs* go unchallenged and reduce esteem even further, they need to offer affirmative alternatives: "We'll tell you what's right about you and what there is to love about you. Disappointment and hurt are not good reasons to decide to think badly about yourself."

If the child starts isolating, acting like a social reject because of feeling rejected, and turning down invitations to go out, then parents need to speak up. Rather than let this negative *treatment* go unchallenged and reduce esteem even further, they need to encourage affirmative alternatives: "Even though you don't feel like it, we think it would do you good to go to the movie with your friends. The better you treat yourself, the better you'll feel about yourself."

Attitude toward self, beliefs about self, and *treatment of self* are three categories of choice that the child controls that most influence his or her self-esteem. When hard life experience makes it difficult for the child to preserve self-worth, parents need to be there to help shore up the child. They need to help the child avoid the trap that lowering self-esteem can set:

- Giving up on oneself
- Beating up on oneself
- Deciding one doesn't deserve taking good care of oneself

They want to give the child this message: "Particularly when life gets hard, we want you to keep a positive attitude, believe good things about yourself, and treat yourself well because your self-esteem depends on it." Parents say this both to give support and provide protection, knowing that *the lower the child's self-esteem, the higher the risk of substance abuse should use occur, and the higher the self-esteem, the lower that risk becomes.*

19

〰〰〰〰〰〰〰〰〰〰〰〰〰〰〰〰〰〰〰〰〰〰〰〰

ADOLESCENCE

PARENTING AGAINST THE
RISK RECEPTORS

The role that adolescence plays in substance use is a major one because most involvement with drugs and alcohol begins not in childhood, but during that eight-to twelve-year period of growth that transforms the dependent child into an independent adult.

Important in helping their son or daughter remain or become substance-free is understanding the nature of adolescence well enough to recognize the developmental risks that make adolescents *emotionally receptive* to drug and alcohol consumption, and then *to parent against those risk receptors.*

This Key explores several emotional receptors built into the larger *phases* of adolescence. The four following Keys look more closely at additional receptors specific to each *stage* of adolescence—Early Adolescence, Mid-Adolescence, Late Adolescence, and Trial Independence.

The Larger Phases of Adolescence

One way to begin understanding the overall process of adolescence is to break it down into *three large sequential phases*:

- The Separation from Childhood
- The Redefinition of Identity
- The Departure into Independence

During each phase, the adolescent typically asserts a new set of developmental differences that create a certain emotional vulnerability for the teenager to manage.

Phase One: The Separation from Childhood and the Receptor of Loneliness

With the assertion of more *oppositional differences*, the boy or girl, through rebellious words and actions, signifies that the separation from childhood has begun.

- "I am *different* from how I was as a child."
- "I wanted to be treated *differently* from when I was a child."
- "I am *different* from how you are as my parents."
- "I am going to be *different* from how you want me to be."

There are two problems with asserting these statements of differentness. First, because they are *oppositional*, the adolescent now fits less harmoniously into family; the boy or girl is at risk of getting into more disagreements and receiving more disapproval within the system ("How many times do we have to ask you to get something done?"). And second, when parents express intolerance of some of these differences, and oppose the child's behavior to show they have had all the differentness they can accept ("No dyed hair!"), the adolescent can feel alienated from authorities who run the system. In consequence of feeling more criticized by and in conflict with parents, the adolescent can feel outcast and *lonely* at home.

During the separation from childhood, loneliness can make the adolescent more receptive to substance use. At this point, the boy or girl is at higher risk of joining friends in substance use to gain a sense of social belonging missed at home. *To parent against this receptor,* parents need to keep communicating acceptance of the adolescent when they are given more cause to take issue with his or her oppositional behavior. They need to continually reach out to *include* him or her in family functions despite the boy or girl's disinterest or outright objections, and they need to continue to voice approval for what they value and appreciate in their son or daughter. *When parents withdraw in frustration, isolation and exclusion can increase the adolescent's loneliness within the family, raising the risk of going along with substance use to belong with friends, or even resorting to substance use when alone.*

What not *to say*: "If you don't want to be with us, then we don't want to be with you."

What to say: "Even though you don't feel like it, we want you to join us and come along."

Phase Two: The Redefinition of Identity and the Receptor of Self-consciousness

With the assertion of *trial differences*, the boy or girl, through words and actions, signifies that the redefinition of identity has begun. Obvious change becomes a regular occurrence. Tastes in appearance, dress, cultural heroes, music, relationships, interests, and aspirations can each be all-important one day and become unimportant the next. "Just 'cause I have lots of clothes that fit my body doesn't mean I have any that fit how I want to look!"

Beholding these changing images, parents can get impatient with the fickle nature of some and the enduring presence of others. In both cases, however, these are trial, not terminal, differences that allow the adolescent to try on and off a host of different ways of being, behaving, and believing, and, in the process, sorting out just who he or she authentically is. To be so changeable and to be caught in the age of in-between—no longer quite a child but not yet quite an adult—is to feel awkward and filled with *self-consciousness*.

During the redefinition of identity, acute self-con-sciousness can make the child more receptive to substance use. To escape this discomfort, particularly with peers, the adolescent is at risk of relying on chemical courage to cover up feelings of insecurity with the appearance of bravado. *To parent against this receptor*, parents need to respect the adolescent's often clumsy efforts at transformation, taking them seriously, showing interest in them, and not dismissing or correcting them in a demeaning way. *Treating trial differ-ences with ridicule, sarcasm, or any humor of the put-down kind raises the risk of injuring fragile self-image with humiliation, which can make the adolescent feel more inclined to medicate or escape painful embarrassment to feel okay.*

What not *to say*: "Do you call that noise music?"

What to say: "Tell me about the group you are listening to."

Phase Three: The Departure into Independence and the Receptor of Loss

With the assertion of *autonomous differences*, the young person, through words and actions, signifies that the departure into independence has begun. Now plans and preparations and the first steps toward living more independently are underway. "I'm ready to go!" declares the adolescent, soon discovering that he or she is really not, because some part of the young person doesn't want to leave.

It is an irony not lost on parents to see their son or daughter, at the point of departure from home and family, suddenly realize the importance of home and family. It will be many years before the adult child develops an independent living place as historically powerful as home, and a set of caring relationships as meaningful as family. Out of this awareness, the young person, departing into independence, confronts the fearful issue of *loss*.

A desire to hold on grips the young person just as he or she is supposed to let go, and scary questions come to mind. Once gone, will he or she be missed? Having left, will he or she now be left out of family life? Will no longer being a daily presence mean being forgotten? In response to this last question, the young person may take steps to secure the place that is being left behind. "Just 'cause I'm not there, you leave my room alone!" And possessions may be stored for years to mark one's place, to show one still belongs.

Preserving one's room, storing one's stuff, coming by for meals, and calling if away (why that first year at college can be so expensive) all are means of staying connected when separated from family. Fear of loss of place in home and family can create enormous insecurity. "Suppose I go so far away, I can't return? Then if I get in trouble, I'll have no safety net to fall back on, no home to come home to!"

When parents treat their son or daughter's departure into independence as giving up all rights to residency at home, they increase the young person's social dependence on peers at a time when insecurity and substance use are destabilizing many young people's lives. *During the departure into independence, fear of loss of place at home can make a child more receptive to substance use.*

What not *to say*: "From now on, you won't live here anymore."

What to say: "For as long as we have a home, you will always have a welcome place to stay should you want to visit or should a temporary need or want arise."

Because risk of involvement with substances is heightened by emotional receptors built into the adolescent process, it is important to parent against those receptors as follows:

- To parent against *loneliness*, focus on *inclusion*, not exclusion.

- To parent against *self-consciousness*, focus on *respect*, not ridicule.

- To parent against *loss*, focus on still *belonging*, not being cut off.

20

EARLY ADOLESCENCE (AGES 9–13)
THE RECEPTOR OF DISAPPROVAL

E arly adolescence is about letting the bad child out. As intended here, "bad" doesn't mean evil, immoral, or illegal acting, just more difficult to live with than the boy or girl was before. "Bad" simply describes how the boy or girl, to differentiate from the more manageable child he or she used to be, now tends to act in ways parents find more objectionable. Come adolescence, there are so many adjectives that describe common behavior changes in their son or daughter with which parents must now contend. The early adolescent may have become more restless, bored, discontent, irritable, inattentive, forgetful, distracted, disorganized, nervous, silly, complaining, uncooperative, critical, oppositional, or challenging, to name a few. No wonder parental attitudes can begin to change in response.

The Receptor of Disapproval

For the child, parental approval counted for a lot. "Watch me!" "What did you think?" "How did I do?" "Do you like what I did?" "Did you like how I did it?" For the early adolescent, however, parental *dis*approval in some ways counts for more. Why? Because parental disapproval provides recognition that the boy or girl is seeking. By noticing his or her change for the worse, they certify that a significant alteration has occurred. "You used to be so happy and well-behaved, what's happened to you? Why are you acting different?" they ask. Answers the early adolescent: "Because I'm not a child anymore!"

Three Stages of Early Adolescence

Three sequential changes identify the onset of early adolescence, each unwelcome to parents in its own way.

1. The negative attitude

2. Rebellion

3. Early experimentation

The negative attitude is the psychological change that starts the engine of adolescence going—the "bad attitude" that parents often find so hard to endure. "He used to be so positive and full of energy. Now all he does is lay around and gripe about having nothing to do, or about something wrong with us. He's so restless and dissatisfied all the time. He's become the family critic, and nothing we can say or do seems to make him happy. What's the matter with him, anyway?"

Adolescence begins when the boy or girl rejects the old identity and treatment that went with being a child, and begins the quest for an older definition that is yet to be determined. The early adolescent knows how she *doesn't* want to be defined and be treated any longer, but has no idea of a positive alternative to put in its place. Hence, for awhile, negativity rules.

Then, dissatisfaction with the past is coupled with another dissatisfaction with the present. Now parents and other adult authorities get in the way of freedom that the child wants in order to grow. In frustration and anger at being pushed by demands and blocked by limits, she may let out her grievance: "It's not fair! What gives you the right to tell me what I can and cannot do? You're not the boss of the world!" *It is this negative attitude that provides the motivation for adolescent change*, driven by dissatisfaction with remaining a child and with being told what to do by adults, preparing the way for the second stage of early adolescence.

Rebellion is impelled by a feeling of *just cause*, and now the adolescent has grievances aplenty: against having nothing to do, against not knowing what to do, against demands that interfere with independence, against limits that prevent freedom, and against having to live on other people's terms.

Two forms of rebellion now frustrate parents, testing their patience and resolve. Through *active resistance*, the boy or girl challenges and disagrees with what parents explain, order, or ask. "He'll even argue about the time of day!" And through *passive resistance*, the boy or girl puts off compliance so parents have to nag and nag to get anything done. "She'll delay us to death!"

It is through rebellion that the boy or girl gathers the power to change, preparing the way for the third stage of early adolescence.

Early experimentation exploits new freedom that rebellion has grudgingly been granted. At least occasionally, the active and passive resistance have caused weary parents to relax their rules or back off their demands. With this success in mind, the early adolescent begins to test other limits and seeks to satisfy a growing curiosity about the world, particularly activities allowed to adults but forbidden to the young.

This is when mischief and early rule breaking can occur (playing pranks, vandalism, shoplifting) that parents must confront with consequences, or more serious offenses are likely to follow. (Thus, parents make sure that the child encounters the victim of their mischief, is told how the victim feels, and perhaps arranges some form of restitution.) This is also a time when freedom for new experience can be taken in unauthorized ways (lying and sneaking out). All these adventures have a common goal: to see what one can get away with, and to see what the world has to offer. *It is through early experimentation that the boy or girl begins to gather the experience to change.*

The Dangers of Parental Disapproval

Although a measure of parental disapproval is satisfying to the early adolescent, affirming growth change that has occurred, *the risk of excessive parental disapproval is that the boy or girl can use it to justify resorting to substances at each stage of the way.*

- *The negative attitude:* no longer wanting to treat themselves, or be treated, as children, *early adolescents may see substance use as a grown-up thing to do.* (And use of tobacco can begin.) To parent against this receptor, parents are often well advised to provide alternative grown-up experiences and responsibilities of which they approve. "Now that you are ready to act older, we want you to have more choice in some of the decisions we used to make for you."

- *Rebellion:* no longer wanting to live on terms set by adult authority, *early adolescents may see substance use as a defiant thing to do.* (And use of alcohol can begin.) To parent against this receptor, parents are often well advised to support challenges as an antidote to rebellion, so that instead of reacting dependently against what parents want, early adolescents are encouraged to act independently for what they want for themselves. "You pick out a sport or other interest you want to try, and we'll support you as our time and money allow."

- *Early experimentation:* no longer willing to live within the old limitations of childhood and curious about the larger world, *early adolescents see substance use as an exploratory thing to do.* (And use of inhalants can begin.) To parent against this receptor, parents are often well advised to listen to, instead of immediately censuring, the boy or girl's interest in, or experience with, the forbidden. Then, they can rationally describe specific dangers of such experimentation and suggest why those risks may not be worth the rewards. "We can't make your choices for you, but we can try to inform your choices by raising possible consequences, so in ignorance you don't get hurt. Inhalants can be extremely dangerous. They can harm your heart rate and your ability to breathe. And they can do permanent damage to major organs like your heart, lungs, and brain."

21

~~~~~~

MID-ADOLESCENCE (AGES 13–16)

THE RECEPTOR OF IMMEDIACY

Mid-adolescence is about a changed attitude toward freedom. For the early adolescent, insufficient personal freedom was primarily a source of injustice to argue about. "Why should I?" and "Why can't I?" generated increasing amounts of dispute. For the mid-adolescent, however, personal freedom is less a matter of grievance to be complained about than an urgent goal to be obtained. The mid-adolescent is intent on doing whatever is necessary—from engaging in elaborate deception to initiating intense conflict—to get the social independence that he or she must have.

The Receptor of Immediacy

"Must" is the operational word for the age because *immediate gratification* is what matters most. A *tyranny of now* prevails as each want is treated as an emergency. "I absolutely have to go!" "If you don't let me, my life is ruined!" "This is more important than anything!" And the mid-adolescent is being honest. Emotionally, it feels like a deferred or denied want has life-threatening costs, cutting off freedom to grow when energy to grow is at its most intense. For the child, patience was easier to bear than for the mid-adolescent, for whom waiting is torment not to be endured.

Three Protections for Freedom of Immediacy

Three strategies for preserving freedom of immediacy tend to characterize mid-adolescence, each creating its own kind of problem for parents: *evasiveness, explosiveness,* and *impulsiveness.*

Evasiveness enables the boy or girl to avoid being talked to, hence, to avoid hearing and responding to parental concerns that might get in freedom's way. It's as though the teenager has decided: "If they can't communicate with me, they can't control me." "The way to keep my freedom is to keep my parents from discussing what I'm going to do."

A number of common tactics are used to discourage parental communication.

- Protective irritation: "Not now, can't you see I'm in a bad mood?"

- Protective busyness: "Not now, can't you see I'm doing something important?"

- Protective unavailability: "Not now, I've got to leave or I'll be late."

- Protective promises: "Not now, we can talk about it when I get back."

The intent of evasion is to free the mid-adolescent to follow the dictates of urgency by creating no good time to talk. Thus, parents have to understand: *a bad time is often going to be the best time to talk, and that's okay.*

Explosiveness enables the boy or girl to lose control to get control of conflict with parents, hence, getting them to give in to freedoms with which they do not actually agree. It's as though the teenager has decided: "Any means in conflict is okay, as long as I get my way." "If they don't want to get hurt, they shouldn't try to keep me from what I want."

Instead of adhering to a rule of safety in family conflict (managing disagreement over differences so no one gets hurt), the mid-adolescent may resort to threatening or committing verbal or physical harm (inflicting injury to win at all costs). The intent of explosiveness is to make the price of conflict so high that parents back off from bringing up what the boy or girl doesn't want to have discussed. Thus, parents have to hang tough. *They will bring up what needs to be talked about whether the boy or girl wants to discuss it or not; and they will insist that the communication is managed in a manner that is safe and respectful for everyone.*

Impulsiveness enables the boy or girl to live freely in the moment with no thought of past constraint or future concern. It's as though the teenager has decided: "There is no time but the present." "Anything worth waiting for is worth having now."

Instead of operating within a framework of responsibility that connects time present to past commitments and future obligations, the mid-adolescent would rather be ruled by a sense of spontaneity. This is particularly true when in the company of friends, where life is governed by group decisions made on the spur of the moment.

In contrast to the child, who was more able to make and stick to plans, the mid-adolescent wants to go with the flow, living unrestricted and unrehearsed. To protect this freedom for immediacy, *vagueness* is often used with parents to keep options from being closed down.

- "What are you going to do?" ask the parents. "Hang out," replies the teenager.

- "Where will you be?" ask the parents. "Around," replies the teenager.

- "Who will you be with?" ask the parents. "Friends," replies the teenager.

- "When will you be back?" ask the parents. "Later," replies the teenager.

In addition to requiring more specifics and pinning down the slippery young person, parents also need to hold the boy or girl accountable: *"If you break a past commitment or face a future difficulty because of how you have behaved in the present, then you must face the consequences of your actions."*

The Dangers of Immediacy

Once the early adolescent has challenged the justice of old restraints, freedom in pure form of immediacy becomes what the mid-adolescent craves. Unfortunately, the risks of this appeal create a powerful vulnerability to the use of substances. *In addition to their mood- and mind-altering effect, most substances create an intense in-the-moment experience, much to be desired.*

Under the influence of LSD, for example, time seems to stop as the most mundane reality is absorbed in distorted and fascinating detail. In inhaling a "popper," an immediate sense of intoxication creates a powerful high with which ordinary experience cannot compete. Experiential immediacy created by substance use can even confuse an older person about how he or she is actually spending time. Consider the story about the young man who got high on speed for two days in order to complete a college paper, finally coming down only to discover to his horror that all he had written, over and over and over again, was the same single opening sentence. Every moment had been a new beginning.

115

Countering the Risks of Substance Use from Immediacy

Evasiveness, explosiveness, and impulsiveness can each, in its own way, serve as an encouragement to substance use.

- Evasiveness: *substance use can offer the boy or girl a way to avoid facing up to hard reality.* In response, parents can make it absolutely clear that drug or alcohol use will not be allowed to put off hard issues or make them go away.

- Explosiveness: *substance use can empower the boy or girl with freedom from emotional restraint when conducting conflict.* In response, parents can insist that the rules of safe conduct in family conflict will be observed, and that explosiveness will not cause parents to abandon taking healthy stands.

- Impulsiveness: *substance use can liberate the boy or girl, creating an experience totally focused in the present, free from any past or future concerns.* In response, parents can let the child know that no impulsive acts are ever truly free because all have consequences that often get worse in proportion to the amount of forethought that has been given up.

22

LATE ADOLESCENCE (AGES 16–18)
THE RECEPTOR OF ANXIETY

L *ate adolescence is about getting ready for independence.* Approaching the age when high school ends and a further step out into the world will soon be taken, the late adolescent has a mixed response to the next degree of freedom—living more on one's own terms. On the one hand, the older teenager is excited by the prospect of living free from parental surveillance and interference, but on the other, he or she feels anxious.

Is the young man or young woman ready for the separation and responsibility that more independence brings? The answer, of course is "No," because no matter how thorough the parenting preparation, it is going to be insufficient to meet all the challenges ahead. Significant knowledge will be lacking, significant skills will be wanting, significant experience will be missing, and significant discipline will be undeveloped.

All of which is okay, because about 60 percent readiness for independence is about the best parents can hope for. The late adolescent has to pick up the balance from the Big R—Reality—through the trial-and-error learning that opportunity and adversity provide. If parents and the late adolescent wait to separate until he or she is entirely ready for independence, separation will never begin. For the young man or young woman, the courage of late adolescence is to

117

leave partly unprepared, and the courage of parents is to let the unprepared young person go.

The Receptor of Anxiety

Anxiety at the point of departure is natural for both the late adolescent and parents because the child's lack of readiness concerns them all. As parental responsibilities for their son or daughter begin to appreciably diminish, those of the young man or young woman become frighteningly real—for bill paying, for holding down a job, for money making and money spending decisions, for education, and for self-management in a host of ways that parents had helped take care of before.

Whereas the early adolescent complained as a matter of principle when full freedom was denied, the late adolescent wouldn't mind delaying some of that independence as a matter of practicality. It feels like too much responsibility too soon, particularly in light of some common fears a young person faces upon graduating high school. Fear from loss of the familiar combines with fear of challenges ahead. What losses? Consider just a few.

- *Loss of friends:* now making of a new social circle must begin as old friends scatter to different destinations and begin to follow different paths in life.

- *Loss of home:* now leaving home becomes more of a possibility or a reality, and as it does, the security of family becomes more strongly missed.

- *Loss of support:* now some loss of parental care is the price for more independence that must be paid.

- *Loss of effectiveness:* now the relative level of competence attained in high school will be more difficult to repeat out in the larger world where comparable recognition is harder to achieve.

No wonder the late adolescent is anxious. To quote one young person: "It feels like starting over!"

Three Insecurities of Late Adolescence

Three insecurities can bedevil a young person at this departure point: from *doubt,* from *confusion,* and from *guilt.* In response, parents need to beware their feelings of ambivalence at this trying time and avoid giving double messages that can place the late adolescent in a painful bind.

Doubt arises when fear erodes confidence, with the young man or young woman wondering: "Will I be able to separate from family and stand alone?" Courage is going forward when confidence is lacking. Parents need to avoid the double message: "We want you to be independent, but we're not sure you can make it on your own." Instead, an expression of faith would help: "We believe you have what it takes to learn independence."

Confusion arises when lack of direction creates fear of an undetermined future. Courage is going forward when you don't know which way to go. Parents need to avoid the double message: "We want you to make your own choices, but we don't want you to make the wrong ones." Instead, acceptance of uncertainty would help: "It takes exploring, and trial-and-error learning, for people to figure out what they want to do in life."

Guilt arises from feeling that departure is partly desertion, abandoning obligation to parents. Courage is going forward when loved ones are left behind. Parents need to avoid the double message: "We want you to go, but you are leaving us alone after all we have done for you." Instead, freeing departure from obligation would help: "Although we will miss you, we will continue to have a satisfying life of our own."

The Danger of So Much Anxiety

Letting go of old associations with high school friends, letting go of traditional reliance on family, and facing new challenges and uncertainties that more independence from home creates can all cause a degree of apprehension that the late adolescent may use substances to quell.

Entering college students, for example, may face considerable anxiety coping with the demands of college life and trying to establish some kind of home away from home for the first time. Without the support of friends and family, in an unfamiliar academic setting, and not yet befriended in a meaningful way, young men and young women can resort to substances to help make them fit in and socially belong.

For some young men entering a fraternity, drinking to get drunk may be more than an initiation rite. It may become an ongoing part of socially performing as a man. Signs of excessive drinking can even become apparent: insomnia (the inability to stay asleep), mood swings, or depression. For some young women entering a sorority, taking a self-prescribed regimen of diet pills (stimulants to diminish appetite) may be more than doing one's best to make a good first impression. It may become an ongoing part of maintaining attractiveness as a woman. Signs of excessive use of diet pills can even become apparent: mood swings, nervousness, and depression.

Relying on the support of substances to reduce late adolescent anxiety can create more difficulties than it solves.

• By not addressing the problem directly itself and by using substances to self-medicate it, anxiety tends to intensify over time. "The more I depend on diet pills to curb my appetite, the more frightened of being overweight I become." Thus, parents can say: "Running away increases fear, and insecurity is worsened when substances alone are used to make it better. Maybe some counseling to deal with your anxiety would help."

- By regularly resorting to substances to cope with an anxiety-provoking situation, a pattern of habituation may become established. "I got used to heavy drinking in college to fit in with my crowd. But when I got out and stopped partying, I couldn't shake the habit." Thus, parents can say: "Although it is easier to make a habit than to break one, since habits are started by choice, choice can also stop them. Maybe you could use a support group like Alcoholics Anonymous (AA) to help make the choice you want."

23

~~~~~~

TRIAL INDEPENDENCE (AGES 18–23)

THE RECEPTOR OF INADEQUACY

T rial independence is about establishing social separation from family and becoming self-supporting. What the late adolescent feared to some degree comes true: the task of successfully assuming independence is too much for most anyone to master right away. For many young people, there is a periodic sense of not measuring up to the task.

- There is so much more to learn than was known before.
- There is so much more demand than one had to keep up with before.
- There is so much more freedom of choice than one was given before.
- There is so much more responsibility than was ever carried before.
- There is so much more social distraction than one had to contend with before.

Surrounded with a cohort of peers who are equally overwhelmed, most young people go through periods of playing at the expense of taking care of business, of slipping and sliding as they try to gain a stable footing, and of drifting aimlessly for want of a clear purpose in life.

The Receptor of Inadequacy

In the process of trying to get independence organized, a host of commitments that support responsibility may be broken: personal promises, bill obligations, credit arrangements, apartment leases, local statutes of various kinds, job contracts, and educational requirements, to name a few. Unfortunately, confusing this period even further is an unhappy reality: *the three to five years after high school tend to be the most drug and alcohol intense, and for that reason may make the final stage of adolescence the most dangerous of all.*

The supply of and demand for substances at this time are extremely high, with hard drugs (like cocaine, heroin, and speed) often more in evidence than before, although alcohol, marijuana, and tobacco still remain the substances of most abuse. Young people, coping with more freedom than they've had before, with the opportunity for partying daily available, are now a more open market than ever because they are no longer protected by the limits of living at home.

To parents, who had expected a twenty-one-year-old to be able to act mature, incidents of irresponsibility can be disturbing: "We thought our child would be acting all grown up by now." But their disappointment is only half of the story. The other half is told by their child: "What's wrong with me? Why can't I just get my life together?" In trial independence, feelings of *inadequacy* can seriously undermine self-esteem.

Three Vulnerabilities of Trial Independence

A young person acting unwisely and suffering a setback during trial independence can injure his or her self-esteem by encouraging feelings of inadequacy in three ways: by *criticism*, by *worry*, and by *despair*.

123

- The *criticism* can be: "What's the matter with me?"
- The *worry* can be: "What's going to happen to me if I keep going on this way?"
- The *despair* can be: "This just goes to show that I'll never learn!"

Having found himself or herself guilty on one or more of these counts of inadequacy, self-doubts can be made worse if parents direct similar charges at their son or daughter themselves.

- They may point out their child's failings with criticism: "What's the matter with you?"
- They may predict worse to come with worry: "What's going to happen to you if you keep going on this way?"
- They may advise giving up by echoing his or her despair: "This just goes to show that you'll never learn!"

If there is one golden rule for parents to follow during their child's bumpy passage through trial independence, it is this: *refrain from expressions of criticism, worry, and despair* because their son or daughter is prone to those responses already. Rather than making their child's vulnerability worse, they are better served, and so is their son or daughter, by providing emotional support.

- Instead of criticism, give an expression of *encouragement:* "Just because you didn't do it right the first time doesn't mean you can't get it right the next."
- Instead of worry, give a vote of *confidence:* "This experience will only make you wiser in the years ahead."
- Instead of despair, give a statement of *faith:* "We believe you have what it takes to find your footing and your way."

The Dangers of Inadequacy

Significant feelings of inadequacy on the threshold of young adulthood can cause a young person to seek escape or solace in substances. Chemical dependence at this age, for example, may be linked to felt incapacity to achieve functional adult independence. If a young person, in this case, has tried a variety of substances earlier in life, a hard drug like heroin, with its deadly peril of overdose, may become a later choice at this time.

Unfortunately, the lifestyle demands of heroin use typically makes functional independence harder to attain. Having to support a heroin habit that craves being fed three or four times a day (to stay high and to avoid withdrawal) means that holding a nine-to-five job is almost impossible. This inability to commit to an eight-hour work day, plus the expenses required to keep buying the drug, often causes a young person to engage in illegal activities to support the addiction. In consequence, instead of life coming together during the final stage of adolescence, life can seriously fall apart.

What can help at the outset of trial independence, before the young person has moved away from home, is for parents to openly acknowledge the challenge of learning independence and to create an acceptance of the task that lays ahead. To parent against the receptor of inadequacy, parents can explain: "Not being able to master independence right after moving out on your own is not a problem. It is simply a reality that you need to accept. What counts at this time is not preparation as much as determination—being able to maintain sufficient momentum to get up after you fall, to keep trying after you fail, and to keep going forward despite feeling discouraged. Keep up your determination, and you will learn what you need to know."

24

~~~~~~

GROUNDS FOR SUSPICION

SIGNS OF SUBSTANCE USE
TO LOOK FOR

How are parents to tell the difference between the normal, albeit more intense, changes that often accompany adolescent growth, and those changes that may signify harmful involvement with substances? *It's not always easy.*

Parents can sometimes discount signs of drug use as typical adolescent behavior ("All teenagers forget to keep their promises."), and at other times can attribute typical adolescent behavior to substance use ("There's something wrong, the way she wants to argue all the time."). On balance, it's probably better to make the second error than the first—to falsely accuse the child and to risk hurt feelings in response than to overlook the truth and let self-destructive behavior continue. So, when in doubt, speak out: "Were use of alcohol or drugs involved in the accident?"

Overlapping and Nonoverlapping Signs of Substance Use

Discriminating the telltale behaviors of adolescence from involvement with substances can be difficult because many of the changes are so similar. Therefore, what helps is if parents can distinguish between *overlapping* (confusing) and *nonoverlapping* (clarifying) signs—those where the difference is hard to tell, and those where substance use is pretty likely.

First, consider some *overlapping signs*. Although substance use tends to intensify adolescent change, not all intense adolescent change is due to substance use. However, multiple (eight to ten), disruptive occurrences of the "normal" changes listed below should cause parents to be more attuned to the possibility that substances *might* be involved.

- Unpredictable mood swings
- Less willingness to communicate; demanding more private time at home
- More volatile in conflict; more depressive when sad
- Dress, room decor, and tastes in music have more drug connotations and content
- Less cooperative at home
- Manipulative behavior—such as acting deliberately nice or mean to get wants met with parents
- Disinterest in traditional activities and disengagement from old friends
- Altering personal appearance to look "different"
- Less focused, more disorganized and forgetful
- Declining interest in school and falling grades
- More rebellious against rules; more argumentative with authority
- Less inclined to join in family activities and functions
- Daydreaming and inattention
- Urgent concern with the present; unconcern with the future
- More avoidance and evasion of issues that parents want to discuss

The *nonoverlapping signs* of substance involvement are almost never part of normal, healthy adolescent growth. They should be taken seriously by parents, particularly if several seem to fit the description of their teenager's behavior.

- Money, or valuables that can be pawned for money, missing from other family members

- Regularly caught smoking cigarettes

- Drug paraphernalia, like rolling papers, pipes, clips, tubes, foil, butane lighters, for example, found among the child's belongings; or empty bottles, canisters, or seeds, for example, found in bedroom or car

- Bottles disappear from parents' liquor supply or are diluted; pills missing from psychoactive prescriptions in the medicine chest

- Change in eating and sleeping habits, doing either noticeably more or less

- New friends who avoid introduction, who are not named, who are often older, or who are always met away from home

- Major house rules like curfew and car use continually broken despite promises to the contrary

- Mysterious phone calls received, particularly late at night, and when parents answer, someone hangs up or declines to leave a name

- Teenager seems to lie about inconsequential events; insists on lying about having lied when caught in a lie

- Drug and alcohol-related violations of the law

- Steady decline in school performance, tardiness to class, lack of attendance, homework not turned in, classwork not completed, and conflicts with school authorities

- Decline in physical condition, such as constant fatigue, incidents of acting uncoordinated, unclear speech, confused thinking, bloodshot eyes, run-down appearance, coughing or runny nose with no signs of being sick, unexplained bruises or what appear to be injection marks on the body
- Teenager in possession of unexplained amounts of money
- Dress and person frequently smell of smoke and alcohol
- Asked about possible substance use, teenager overreacts with explosive hostility

The Right to Privacy

Just suppose that sufficient numbers of overlapping and nonoverlapping signs of substance use have been identified by parents to cause them concern, but their son or daughter refuses to answer the questions they ask.

"Anything goes wrong," charges the teenager, "and all you think about are drugs! Well, I'm sick of not being trusted. Just leave me alone!"

Now what are parents supposed to do?

The answer is: use grounds for suspicion to look for harder evidence.

"You searched my room? You took my stash! That's stealing! I could have you arrested! That's violating my right to privacy!"

"No," explain the parents. "Your privacy is a privilege earned by earning our trust; it's not a right. And when you abuse that privilege by using it to conceal destructive and unlawful behavior, we have the right to search and seizure, and that's what we have done. Now, let's talk about what's been going on."

25

~~~~~~

DETECTION

CHECKING OUT SUSPICIONS

How informed about their adolescent son or daughter's life is it realistic to expect parents to be? The answer to this question is influenced by three constraints.

1. Because they have separate lives of their own to lead, parents cannot shadow their teenager 24 hours a day.

2. To get freedom from and freedom for, most adolescents grow up partly outside parental rules and regulations.

3. Few adolescents tell their parents the truth, the whole truth, and nothing but the truth all of the time.

Like it or not, *a considerable amount of ignorance is an unavoidable part of parenting*, particularly during adolescence when parental needs for information increase as their teenager's willingness to fully communicate often declines. At best, parents can hope for sufficient openness to be entrusted with the truth when it is something they should absolutely know.

Unfortunately, because substance use is a legally forbidden activity, and most every teenager knows that parents will disapprove, he or she usually elects to keep it secret, leaving them in the dark. So how are parents to find out? Not able to see the truth (denied *observational data*), and not being told the truth (denied *conversational data*), parents must rely on figuring out the truth from what overlapping and nonoverlapping signs suggest (using *circumstantial data*).

They have to act not on certainty, but on suspicion, playing *detective*, holding their adolescent suspect as they seek clues to explain whatever changes for the worse have occurred. Although most parents don't like having to act in this investigative role, many times this is the only way to find out. Checking, searching, questioning, evaluating inconsistencies, and interviewing other people in their son or daughter's world, and finally pinning down the young person's substance use or determining drugs are not part of the problem.

Substance Use Is Hard to Conceal

A few adolescents are sophisticated enough to conceal significant substance use behind normal outward appearances and behavior, but most cannot. Fearful of being found out, they act atypically secretive and evasive, and their sneakiness gives them away. Becoming self-absorbed in substance use to their cost, they lose some common sense and self-control, making unwise decisions that get them in trouble, and this uncharacteristic stupidity gives them away. *When normally unguarded kids act secretive or when normally smart kids act stupid, parents need to factor in the possibility of problems with substances.*

One assurance that parents can give their child is that on a physical level, most substance use cannot be concealed. *Substances cannot be ingested without, for varying periods of time, creating evidence of their presence as they pass through the young man or young woman's physical system.*

Drug Testing

When a police officer stops a young person on probable cause of driving while intoxicated by alcohol, there are a number of tests that the officer can run to verify this suspicion. In addition to *a field sobriety test* to roughly assess mental or physical impairment, *a breath test* may be given to estimate alcohol content in the blood. If taken into custody, *a blood test* may be given to determine blood alcohol level more precisely (safe driving limits vary by state from up to .08 to .10 milligrams of alcohol per deciliter of blood). *A urine test* can also be given to detect alcohol being metabolized by the liver. Alcohol, however, is only one substance that testing can verify.

"An inexpensive, sensitive laboratory test called chromatography can be used to check . . . (a person's) . . . urine for heroin, morphine, amphetamines, barbiturates, codeine, cocaine, marijuana, methadone, or other phenothiazines." (See Suggested Reading, Merck, p. 1150.) As for marijuana, "urine test results . . . generally remain positive for several days after use, even for casual users. For regular users, test results may remain positive longer while the drug is slowly released from the body fat." (See Suggested Reading, Merck, p. 449.)

One source believes that the value of drug testing goes beyond verification. It can also have preventive value. "Having a urine screen performed is a simple way for you to learn if your kids are in trouble. It also provides a way out for children faced with pressure to use drugs. They can tell their friends that their parents will find out because the doctor tests their urine . . . If you have teenagers, it's a good idea to take them to the doctor at least twice a year for a checkup. And when you do, make it a standard procedure that your doctor request a urine sample. Then be sure the doctor does a drug test. Tell your kids ahead of time that the doctor runs drug tests on adolescents. That way they'll see it isn't just you who is insuring there's no drug problem. If this is done from an early age, it won't cause conflict between you and your children. And if you actually suspect drug use, you can have the doctor perform a more extensive test." (See Suggested Reading, Arterburn and Burns, p. 114.)

At issue is, how far are parents willing to go to evaluate possible substance use by their child? The answer is, it varies widely from family to family—from the overpermissive who would rather not deal with the problem to the overprotective who worry about little else. Some middle ground—sensitive to the possibility but not obsessive about it—is where most parents need to be. The guideline is: when in serious doubt, check it out.

If circumstances cause parents to seriously suspect that substances might be disorganizing their child's life, but the child staunchly denies this possibility, it is perfectly legitimate to get a drug test. If the young person has nothing to hide, then there is no reason for him or her to refuse what he or she will probably not like having to do.

26

CONFRONTATION

FACING THE PROBLEM

D espite all they have been told about the prevalence of substances in the lives of young people growing up today, most parents are still caught off guard when they discover that their child has been using alcohol or drugs. Why? For two reasons:

1. They didn't know, partly because they didn't want to know. (Denial by the parents.)

2. They didn't know, partly because they weren't supposed to know. (Concealment by the child.)

Discovery occurs when one or both—denial or concealment—breaks down. As in most times of family crisis, *what* people have to go through is less important than *how* they go through it, the "how" having to do with the manner in which they communicate with each other. Thus, parental response to discovery can make a difference in the kind of communication that follows—either inflammatory (creating an overreaction ruled by emotional upset) or helpful (creating an interaction ruled by reasonable discussion).

Parents need to anticipate the possibility of their child's substance use, so if it happens, and they find out, they can calmly respond without provoking undue defensiveness in the teenager. No substance use whatsoever throughout the course of adolescence is a worthy objective for their child, but in the majority of cases, it is an unrealistic expectation.

During their growing up, most young people experience some degree of substance use.

Expecting prohibition and punishment to be sufficient to deter their child's drug and alcohol use is probably unrealistic. At most, both give strong statements of disapproval that do inform the child about where parents stand. More powerful parental influences, however, are what parents model in terms of their own substance use, the guidance they give, the understandings they provide, and the open discussions about the subject they are willing to have with the child.

Most important, *their child's substance use is too important for parents to act emotionally upset about,* because *danger* is the point. Because some degree of danger is always associated with any amount of substance use, what the child needs at this time of discovery is parents who can keep a cool head, not lose it. So what are parents supposed to do when discovery occurs? *Confront the problem.*

What Is Meant by Confrontation?

Confrontation means parents speaking up to express an awareness of the child's substance use in a nonjudgmental, direct, matter-of-fact way that their son or daughter is willing to hear and perhaps discuss. Five components of confrontation are:

1. To *describe the data* that have led parents to speaking up, encouraging the child to admit what has specifically been going on. "We found empty bottles hidden in the bottom of the trash last weekend after you had your new friends overnight."

2. To *express concern* to raise the child's concern for his or her own welfare. "We worry that the more you've used, the more run-down you've become."

3. To *raise issues* they want the child to raise for himself or herself. "It's our impression that the only reason you get together with those particular friends is to get high."

4. To *ask questions* they want the child to ask himself or herself. "Do you think those friends would stay your friends if you stopped using?"

5. To *make connections* they want the child to make for himself or herself. "Would you have gotten into that fight if you hadn't been drunk?"

The goal of confrontation is to expand awareness of substance use to allow children to make one or more of several healthy choices:

- To get back on an honest footing with themselves and with parents
- To consider stopping harmful substance use
- To agree to counseling or treatment help if the desire to stop is there, but the capacity is not

Confrontation and Level of Use

Depending on the amount of data that they have, parents can make some initial assessment about the level of their child's use, and tailor questions in the confrontation accordingly.

If the use is *experimental* (using no more than several times out of curiosity), they can ask: "Although we wish you hadn't, now that you've tried it, what did you learn it was like?"

If the use was *recreational* (using on social occasions with peers), they can ask: "Although we wish you hadn't, in the company of friends, were you able to drink just how much you wanted, or did you feel pressured to drink more to keep up with them?"

If the use was *abusive* (using to the point of losing caring and getting in trouble), they can ask: "Although we wish you hadn't, how did starting off the evening to get a buzz on end up with you getting in an accident?"

If the use was *addictive* (using to support psychological or physical dependence), they can ask: "Although we wish you hadn't, what kind of need caused you to steal from your own parents, pawn what you stole, to get money to buy a drug that can kill you if you're not careful, and if you get caught can get you thrown in jail?"

The key to successful confrontation is doing it with caring, with specificity, and with patience. This last quality is important because it can take numerous confrontations, if ever, before a substance-abusing or addicted person may be able to take that opportunity and admit the self-destructive pattern of behavior that has become established.

An approach to confrontation that has allowed many addicted people to accept the need for treatment is called *intervention*. One source (See Suggested Reading, Phelps and Nourse, p. 113) summarizes it well: "A structured intervention is a preplanned, rehearsed scenario guided and directed by a professional, in most cases a psychologist, sociologist, or case worker associated with a professional alcoholism treatment center (although interventionists may also be found in private practice). The intervention itself consists of close family members and friends telling the alcoholic at a preappointed time and place, without recrimination or accusation, how much they love the person and how specific elements of his or her alcoholic behavior have been hurting them, one by one, and to offer loving pleas to the alcoholic to go to treatment." The same intervention may work with drug addiction, too.

137

To some degree, all confrontation is an act of courage because it means parents are speaking up for the child's best interests against what he or she wants, or wants to hear. *Confrontation means caring enough to put the child's caring for parents, at least for the moment, at risk, sometimes receiving anger and rejection in return.*

27

▲▲

CHOICE
GIVING THE CHILD THE PROBLEM

When it comes to their child breaking free of substance abuse or addiction, there is a very important reality that parents must accept: *they have no actual control over their child's decision to use, or not to use, alcohol or drugs.* Desperate to save the young person from possible self-destruction, this statement is an unwelcome one because it sounds like saying there is nothing they can do. *Untrue.* It is actually the key to understanding the help that they are empowered to give.

Respecting the Division of Responsibility
When a hard problem like substance abuse or addiction is allowed to blur boundaries of individual responsibility in family relationships, then effective action is *almost impossible* to take. Two sources of great confusion in this situation are usually *blame* and *guilt*. The substance-abusing child often blames parents rather than take responsibility; the guilty parents often blame themselves rather than hold the child accountable.

For the young substance abuser, to blame others is to take on the *victim* role: "If you hadn't fought all those years and gotten divorced, I wouldn't have needed what drugs could give. See what you did to me?" Casting off responsibility for his or her decisions, the young person is reduced to a helpless state. *Without the power to choose, he or she doesn't have the power to change.*

Parents who blame themselves for choices that the child makes take on the *culprit* role: "If we had just been better parents, our child never would have turned to drugs. What did we do wrong? How can we make it right?" By using guilt to claim control of choices not their own, parents presume more power than they actually possess. This encourages the child to give up responsibility, when only by taking it can recovery begin. *If they appropriate ownership of the child's personal choice, the child won't learn responsible self-control.*

Simply because parents have no power to make the child make different choices around substances, however, doesn't mean that by choosing to act differently themselves they can't *influence* choices the child might make. This is the division of responsibility that must be absolutely clear: the child is accountable for his or her behavior, and parents are accountable for theirs. It is by changing their own behavior that parents can begin to help their child. Change how? *By being sure that they are part of the solution, and not part of the problem.*

What Parents Can Stop Doing

Before they can help their drug-abusing or addicted child, parents first have to make sure that they have ceased doing any harm. What harm? Often their well-intentioned efforts to prevent harm from their son or daughter's self-destructive behavior only supports continuation of the very problem they want to stop. *Enabling* is the term used to describe how parents, because they care so much, actually engage in behaviors that help make the problem worse, by protecting their child from paying the costs of his or her drug-affected decisions.

Consider just a few of the common ways enabling is done.

- *By denying reality.* "We only have the word of other parents, and we choose to believe our child."

- *By avoiding conflict.* "If we say anything, that will just cause a fight."

- *By lying for the child.* "This one time, we'll tell the school you were home sick instead of skipping with your friends."

- *By preventing responsibility.* "We'll pay your fine since you don't have the money."

- *By covering up evidence.* "We flushed the stuff away so it can't be used against you."

- *By rationalizing.* "All kids sometimes take money from family when they need it."

- *By treating promises as performance.* "She said she was sorry to be caught and it won't happen again."

- *By rescuing from trouble.* "Of course, we got a lawyer to get the charges dropped."

- *By adjusting to unhealthy behavior.* "We said it's okay to stack beer cans in his room for decoration as long as they are empty."

- *By accepting the unacceptable.* "She only said such terrible things to us because she was all messed up."

- *By defending wrong behavior.* "It wasn't his fault he got busted. The police were just out to make an example of a high school kid."

- *By making exceptions.* "As long as she excels at school, occasionally getting drunk to let off steam on weekends is okay."

- *By making excuses.* "If it hadn't been for other kids and their bad influence, our child would never have tried the stuff."

Giving the Child the Problem

Consequences inform the person choosing about the wisdom of choices made. To save the child from what happened, when substance use impaired judgment and empowered impulse, can be a mistake. Such parental protection short-circuits the connection between choice and consequence that hard experience has to teach.

"But if we let her plead guilty to the Minor In Possession charge, think of the possible costs! There's her reputation. She could think of herself as some kind of criminal. It could affect getting a job if an employer asked about any trouble with the law. It could mean another minor offense would be treated more harshly because of the first. She'd have to be so careful from now on! We can't let one stupid mistake jeopardize her future!"

But that is exactly what parents need to do, because *now is later.* How a child learns to govern himself or herself in the present shapes how he or she will do so in the future. Shield the boy or girl from consequences of unhealthy or unlawful behavior now, and no knowledge is gained to prevent more serious transgressions later on. Parents can allow "community" responses to social transgressions to help teach hard lessons that the child needs to learn.

Essential to a young person's recovery from substance abuse or addiction is the willingness to own personal choice and to face the consequences that followed.

The opposite of enabling is *tough love.* Tough love means loving one's child enough to let him or her get "it," face "it," and deal with "it." "It" is the responsibility connection that links choice and consequence. If parents really want to help their drug-abusing or addicted child toward recovery, then they need to do the child a favor that he or she will *not* appreciate at the time. They need to be able to say something like this: "We respect your right to make your own choices, even those with which we disagree. We also respect your capacity to deal with the consequences. Therefore, *we are turning the problem over to you* and hope you are able to learn some helpful lessons we believe this problem has to teach."

28

~~~~~~

COUNSELING
HELPING PARENTS HELP THE CHILD

The effects of a child's substance abuse and addiction don't seem to make good sense in at least three puzzling ways.

1. Why would a young person want to seek pleasure through a means that brings harm to himself or herself?

2. Why would a young person's individual problem become a family problem?

3. Why would parents, trying their best to make their child's problem better, often only make it worse?

The answer to all three questions is that *substance abuse and addiction are extremely confusing*. The afflicted individual becomes so mixed up that he or she now unwittingly plays by a self-destructive set of rules, often sending mixed messages to parents and creating contradictions that are hard for them to understand.

- What the child says ("I promise I'll stick to curfew") is not the same as keeping one's word (he or she continually comes home late).

- What the child says ("I'm not using drugs") is not exactly what the child means (he or she is "just" using alcohol).

- What the child says ("I didn't do it") is not actually true (he or she did do it).

- What the child says ("I want to get my grades up") is not how the child acts (now spending time on anything but study).

No wonder parents get mixed up too, not knowing what to believe, becoming disorganized, and even counterproductive in response. *When parental confusion reigns, that is usually a sign that the drug-abusing child has too much influence on family functioning.* Competent counseling can help bring clarity and restore healthy structure for parents at a time when a child (drug abusing or not) seems to be careening out of control, unmindful of whatever correction and direction they are trying to impose. For parents to seek counseling help is to admit there is a problem, to realize they do not have the skills and understanding to solve it, and, most important, to recognize that *they do not have to go it alone.*

To find a family counselor knowledgeable about adolescent drug abuse, they can call up their local mental health association, alcohol or drug prevention programs, or local treatment centers or hospitals and get the names of experienced helpers whom these agencies would recommend or regularly refer.

Counseling itself can serve many helpful purposes.

- To provide a regular meeting time when family members can safely talk because the counselor is there to help manage communication, sort out confusion, mediate conflicts, monitor agreements, and predict problems that helpful changes may create

- To support parents taking healthy stands with a child who has too much power for his or her own good in the family, and to support a child who has legitimate concerns to express that parents do not credit or ignore

- To bring in outside resources when necessary, for example, when hospitalization or legal advice is indicated

There is one function of the counselor that is particularly worth emphasizing: *helping parents redefine their role with the child in a healthy way.* Why is this necessary? Because when a child abuses substances, confusing though family life can become, it is predictable in that to some degree, *a harmful role reversal has taken place.* Instead of the child adjusting to the demands of a healthy family system, the family system tends to adjust to unhealthy functioning of the child. Instead of parents initiating and enforcing constructive terms on which the child is supposed to live, increasingly they become reactors, adapting to the destructive terms set by the child.

At this point, *counseling can help restore constructive parenting around the substance-abusing child.* Why is this so important? Because it's very hard for an unhealthy-acting boy or girl to get well in a family system that either models or reinforces its own unhealthy behavior. When parents are helped to replace their confused, inconsistent, and enabling conduct with firm and constructive stands, the afflicted child *is given a healthy set of rules and expectations that he or she can choose to live by.*

Healthy Parenting of a Substance-Abusing Child

Counseling can help parents take stands to oppose three characteristics in their child that tend to gather power as substance use increasingly governs his or her life:

1. The shell of self-centeredness

2. The defense against accountability

3. The refusal to abide authority

To counter each trend can mean encountering conflict because the child will defend unhealthy freedom that he or she has gained, not wanting to give it up.

The shell of self-centeredness that the substance-abusing child develops focuses the boy or girl on *satisfying self by having pleasure now.* At the same time parents accept this driving motivation, they are encouraged by the counselor to do so within limits. To their child they say: "Although satisfying yourself is important, we expect you to also *consider the needs and wants of others.* Although having pleasure is important, we also expect you to sometimes *work before pleasure, in order to earn pleasure.* Although having what you want now is important, we also expect you sometimes to *delay immediate gratification or even do without.*"

The defense against accountability comes into play when, having chosen his or her way into trouble and facing consequences that will limit precious freedom, the substance-abusing child uses communication to create deception by *lying* about what happened, by making *excuses* about what happened, by *denying* that anything happened, or by *blaming* somebody else for what happened. Now parents are encouraged by the counselor to say: "Instead of accepting your lies, *now we expect the truth.* Instead of accepting your excuses, *now we expect you to face what happened.* Instead of accepting your denial, *now we expect admission.* Instead of accepting your blame of others, *now we expect you to take responsibility for your actions.*"

The refusal to abide authority has usually allowed the substance-abusing child to back parents off from healthy structural stands they would normally take, five sources of their social authority losing influence in the process.

1. Instead of making demands, *parents may have abandoned making demands.*

2. Instead of setting limits, *parents may have reneged on limits.*

3. Instead of questioning, *parents may have ignored what they needed to ask.*

4. Instead of confronting difficult issues, *parents may have avoided discussing what mattered.*

5. Instead of allowing or applying negative consequences, *parents may have rescinded promised consequences of their own or may have rescued the child from consequences others have set.*

Now parents are encouraged by the counselor to say: "There will be times when *we will make demands* for you to do what you don't want to do, and *we expect you to comply.* There will be times when *we will set limits* on your freedom that prevent you from doing what you want, and *we expect you to obey.* There will be times when *we will ask questions* that you would rather ignore, and *we expect you to truthfully and fully answer.* There will be times when *we will confront you* on issues that you would rather avoid, and *we expect you to be willing to discuss* them. There will be times when *we will let you take your consequences,* and *we expect you to take full responsibility* for the bad choices that you have made."

Outside counseling to help restore healthy parenting around the substance-abusing child often is enough to encourage the boy or girl to begin to behave in self-corrective ways. If however, after several months of counseling, significant improvement is not achieved, or the child's behavior and evidence of use gets clearly worse, then more intensive help—out-patient or in-patient treatment—should be considered.

29

^^^

TREATMENT

WHEN OUTSIDE COUNSELING IS NOT HELP ENOUGH

A lthough convincing themselves to seek counseling can be difficult (admitting to a family problem they cannot solve alone), taking the step toward getting treatment can be harder still for parents. Feeling defensive, they may ask themselves: "What does it say about us to have a child enter treatment?" *The answer is that they care enough about their child and their family to get the help they need.*

What Is Treatment?

Substance abuse, and particularly substance addiction, can adversely affect all areas of a young person's life.

- It can affect how he or she comes to *live within himself or herself* (by engaging in denial and harboring resentment to justify substance use, for example).

- It can affect how he or she comes to *live with others* (by lying and manipulating to achieve exploitive ends, for example).

- It can affect how he or she comes to *live with the world* (by breaking rules and laws to get illicit freedom, for example).

To combat such pervasive and deeply habituated self-destructive behavior is usually more than most parents, even with the aid of counseling, are able to accomplish. They are not up against a problem with a single cause, but one that is determined by many contributing factors: cultural (rebellious attitudes toward authority), social (experiences with substance-using peers), educational (a learned pattern of destructive habituation), psychological (negative beliefs about self), genetic (inherited predisposition to addiction), familial (hurtful dynamics within the home), and physical (in the case of some addictions). To effectively deal with extreme substance abuse or addiction, a more powerful mode of help is required. That help is *treatment*.

The purpose of treatment is to provide a multidimensional, group therapeutic program designed to help young people:

- Interrupt their use of substances and get support for abstaining
- Come to honest terms with the personal costs of their abuse or addiction
- Start recovery of a sober healthy lifestyle independent of any need for alcohol or drugs

Types of treatment vary. The most intensive and expensive is *in-patient* care—in a hospital or residential program. The least intensive and expensive is day or evening *out-patient* care. Therapeutic communities and halfway houses fall somewhere in between. Choice of treatment will partly depend on severity of the child's need, and partly on what parents are able to afford. Upon what does a successful outcome to treatment most depend? *Probably the most important variable affecting how well a program works is how hard the patient works at the program being offered.*

The advantage of in-patient hospital treatment is the collaborative strength of diverse staffing to cope with a complicated problem, the capacity to safely detoxify a young person and assess the physical damage that substances may have done, and the ability to diagnose other physical and psychological problems that may be contributing to the young person's condition. If medical attention is not required, however, then residential treatment may be a good choice. *In-patient care* of either kind removes the young person from his or her social world for several weeks of drug-free living, breaks contact with using peers, simplifies his or her life to focus on the problem, allows for intensive self-evaluation and honest self-expression in therapeutic groups, and creates a time away from home to lower tension, gain perspective, and get family counseling to help adjust those relationships back to health.

One source (see Suggested Reading, Schuckit, p. 161) lists four criteria for choosing in-patient over out-patient care.

1. A previous out-patient treatment didn't work.

2. Medical problems make it advisable for the person to be closely monitored.

3. Depression, anxiety, confusion, or psychotic thinking are severe.

4. Social situations either at home, work, or school are very unstable.

A major advantage of *out-patient care* is that the young person is not working on recovery institutionally removed from his or her social and family world, but is still actively engaged with those daily demands. There is no problem of reentry into social reality that goes with the return from in-patient care, and challenges of coping with the daily stresses and temptations of normal life can be brought into treatment and resolved.

Shopping for the Right Program

In purchasing this mode of health care, parents should shop around, comparing available programs and checking them out before signing up. Get recommendations from knowledgeable helpers in the community. Get references from people who have completed each program who are willing to share what their experience was like. Ask for written materials that describe the scope of the program, interview a staff representative of the program, and expect to get honest, realistic answers to your questions (not a sales presentation or promises that no program can guarantee). Although there are many characteristics to look for in addition to their level of comfort with the program staff they meet, here are five that parents may want to consider.

1. *Longevity and low treatment staff turnover.* In general, older programs with an established approach and proven stability may serve better than ones that may boast newer and fancier facilities.

2. *Utilization of a team approach to treatment.* Because addicts can be extremely confusing and deceptive to help, they need to be outnumbered by a team of people—some of whom may be fooled some of the time, but all of whom are unlikely to be fooled at any one time—able to rely on the collaborative wisdom of each other in assessing and responding to the patient's needs.

3. *A family counseling component in treatment.* Because family relationships have been strained by the young person's substance use and the traditional parental response to it, these relationships need to be repaired. Unaltered family dynamics risk setting the child back when he or she returns home from treatment.

4. *Treatment is linked to a twelve-step recovery program.* Because treatment is just the beginning of a long-term recovery process, it needs to be integrated with the most tested ongoing self-help program yet developed, Alcoholics Anonymous (AA), or one of its derivative support and recovery groups (see Key 30).

5. *Aftercare and relapse recovery programming are provided.* Although many nationally recognized programs have powerful reputations, attending a local community treatment facility has the advantage of offering a continuity of aftercare, which is often essential for the young person's ongoing sobriety and recovery. The problem with faraway programs is that they usually cannot provide this follow-up support in an effective manner, particularly in the case of relapse.

Realistic Expectations

About treatment, there is both good news and bad. The good news is that most problems on the level of substance abuse can be substantially helped. The bad news is that most problems on the level of substance addiction are more intractable, with a far higher likelihood of *relapse*, whereby the young person returns to use after use has been given up (see Key 31).

One source (see Suggested Reading, Phelps and Nourse, p. 123) estimates the success of treatment for one kind of substance addiction, alcoholism, as follows: "The plain fact is that no single approach to treatment works all the time. Although dependable statistics don't exist, there is ample internal evidence to indicate that all approaches yield relatively low-percentage permanent results, less than 50 percent."

For addicted adolescents, treatment is neither a quick fix nor a cure. *No responsible program guarantees to end addiction.* What treatment can be is the beginning of a slow, long process of recovery, as young people are given a chance to stop and consider and learn and change their addictive ways. Once addicted, always addictive is the reality they must come to accept and understand. Then, with ongoing support and continuous effort they can come to live a full and satisfying drug-free life.

30

‹‹‹

SELF-HELP GROUPS

ALCOHOLICS ANONYMOUS AND
THOSE THAT FOLLOWED

When treatment, aftercare, or halfway house time are over, will the chemically dependent young person remain substance-free on his or her own?

In too many cases, the answer is "No." *Going it alone can risk relapsing back to substance use because the old power of habituation and the lure of old companions prove too strong to resist.* What is needed, if treatment change is to translate into lifelong change, is ongoing support to continue recovery. Fortunately, that support is widely available at no cost, thanks to *Alcoholics Anonymous* (AA) and other self-help groups modeled on the AA program, such as *Al-Anon* (for codependent relatives of an alcoholic or drug-addicted family member), *Cocaine Anonymous, Narcotics Anonymous,* or *Overeaters Anonymous* (for people who compulsively overeat in an addictive fashion).

To locate any of these groups in one's own community or nearby, consult the telephone directory. If the young person's drug of choice is not alcohol, a narcotic, or cocaine, then the best group to start attending is AA, using the example of alcohol addiction to understand the workings of one's own substance of abuse (psychological dependence on marijuana, for example).

These self-help groups for various kinds of addictions create a fellowship of people, from all walks of life and with varying years of sobriety, who are trying to live healthy and rewarding drug-free lives *one day at a time*. Through studying group literature, attending meetings, following a twelve-step recovery program, and having and being a sponsor, members come to help themselves by helping each other. Everyone learns from this exchange about the ups and downs of recovery. Because addiction is too psychologically complex for most affected individuals to recover from alone, the twelve-step group can provide a source of invaluable understanding and support, reinforcing the principle of collaboration to cope with human problems: "None of us are as smart as all of us."

The AA program has worked well for many people, helping them remain abstinent and gain recovery of a drug-free life by staying:

- *mentally sane* (keeping a realistic perspective)
- *responsibly honest* (owning the truth to self and others)
- *emotionally sober* (disallowing the rule of fear, resentment, or despondency)
- *spiritually strong* (nourishing a personal faith to rely on)

Treatment and Twelve-Step Groups

Most addiction treatment facilities embrace the twelve-step philosophy, striving to discharge a patient committed to an AA or similar program for future support and further recovery. "Working the steps" (the twelve steps to recovery) over many years is the key, and if a treatment program can get a young person to commit to the first step, it will have done a lot. The first AA step is *admitting* that one is powerless over alcohol and recognizing that one's life has become unmanageable. It is the *delusion* of self-control over use of the substance and *denial* of problems that substance use creates that helps protect and perpetuate addiction. If a young person can reach the admission step, seeing through delusion and dropping denial, then there is a chance for continued abstinence and the opportunity for recovery reinforced by the remaining steps of AA.

Reading this, some parents may wonder that if most treatment is directed toward membership in an AA or similar self-help program, why not get their son or daughter directly into a twelve-step group (which is free) and skip treatment (which is expensive)?

First, many people, young and old, have found sobriety and begun recovery by going directly to AA or its like. So that is always worth a try. If, however, this introduction doesn't take and the young person's substance use becomes worse, then a "time-out to dry out" in treatment to confront the continuing self-destruction may be the wisest choice. Second, where there are medical concerns about physical damage being done, or the possibility of significant other psychological problems (like depression) that need to be assessed, hospitalization may be indicated. And third, for many people, what is learned in treatment provides motivation for a "jump-start on recovery."

Al-Anon—Help for Family Members

One common expectation of parents is that once their child's drug use subsides, his or her problems, and those of the family, will disappear. This belief is unrealistic for a number of reasons.

- Abstinence doesn't make addicted people well, it just gets them sober.

- Substance abuse or addiction partly depends on self-destructive beliefs and self-defeating behaviors that can only begin to be corrected once harmful reliance on drugs or alcohol has stopped.

- When a family member becomes chemically dependent, the whole family, particularly parents, usually become *involved* in the addiction in unhealthy (codependent) ways.

- When unhealthy behavior of the addict interacts with unhealthy behavior of the parents, everyone tends to bring out the worst in each other, and what is the worst for the relationship.

- For a family to get well, both the addicted child and the codependent parents need to each take responsibility for their own destructive functioning and for recovering a healthy way to live within themselves and with each other.

Al-Anon, a twelve-step recovery program originally for spouses of alcoholics, provides a forum where parents, and other family members, can get necessary support and understanding to cope with their substance-addicted child or sibling, and to free themselves from four fateful errors.

1. *Trying to control the addiction:* acting like one has the power to stop another person's use (regularly throwing out cigarettes that are found to keep the child nicotine-free, for example). *In Al-Anon, they learn the importance of letting go what they can't control.*

2. *Enabling the addiction:* actively or passively acting to encourage the addiction (appealing a suspension to protect the addictive child from penalities of being caught with substances at school, for example). *In Al-Anon, they learn the importance of not colluding in the problem by warding off consequences.*

3. *Emotional enmeshment with the addict:* basing one's emotional state on the emotional ups and downs of another person (getting sad and discour-

aged when their addictive child is feeling sad and discouraged, for example). *In Al-Anon, they learn the importance of emotional detachment.*

4. *Self-sacrifice for the addict:* focusing on another person's needs to the extent that one's own are neglected (giving up a planned vacation in order to stay home just in case there is another crisis in their addictive child's life, for example). *In Al-Anon, they learn the importance of self-care.*

Twelve-step programs do not work for everyone, nor are they the only self-help groups available to provide support. As of this writing, however, Alcoholics Anonymous and those that use its model are the most widely available and time tested. Which kind of support group should people use? Whichever works best for them.

31

RECOVERY

"PROGRESS, NOT PERFECTION" (AA)

Parents need to be realistic about recovery—the process of achieving sobriety and learning to live in a healthy and rewarding drug-free way. *Living in recovery is very hard for the addicted young person to do.*

1. It requires denying the pleasure center in the brain those good feelings it has come to crave. *Giving up drugs means giving up pleasure.*

2. It requires changing one's habit of socializing with other people that regularly use substances. *Giving up drugs means giving up friends.*

3. It requires confronting who and how one really is. *Giving up drugs means giving up dishonesty for truth.*

4. It requires meeting the demands of life without depending on substances to cope. *Giving up drugs means giving up chemical support.*

5. It requires rearranging one's life to exclude, instead of to accommodate, the use of drugs. *Giving up drugs means giving up the comfortable for the unfamiliar.*

6. It requires experiencing life without anesthetizing emotion. *Giving up drugs means giving up self-medicating pain.*

Considering all these sacrifices, recovery is not quick or easy. And it is not certain. Because the door to old addictive compulsions can never be locked, the attainment of recovery can never be secure. Slipping back into incidental use, even *relapsing* into an old pattern of addiction, are always possibilities of which the recovering addict (of any age) must be constantly aware.

The price of freedom (in this case, from falling back into addiction) is remaining ever mindful of one's addiction. This is why living one day at a time in a twelve-step program is so helpful. It reminds people of the addictive risk at which they must always live. It keeps them from getting complacent, "graduating" from the daily danger, acting like it's over, and then falling off the path of recovery. At best, addiction is only in abeyance within them, a problem that can be successfully treated, but not cured.

Because of all that must be given up for the sake of abstinence and recovery, the pain from loss can be profound. "I felt better off when I was getting high, even though it messed me up and bought me a bunch of trouble. I mean, give it up and what do you get? Strung out, and now my getaway is gone! This is the toughest thing I've ever done!" Yes, it probably is. Getting on drugs is infinitely easier than getting off.

The rewards of recovery (improved health and self-esteem, among them) do not come right way. Feeling worse before you start feeling better is how sobriety begins. The young person who recalled how "early recovery was a pain" was telling the truth. It is a very difficult time. A lot of support is usually required to successfully get over the hump; hence, the AA advice to newly sober members: *attend ninety meetings in ninety days.*

Addiction—Involuntary Condition and Voluntary Choice

People do not choose to become addicted. Addiction is multiply determined by social, cultural, and physiological factors over many of which the young person has no control. Some percentage of substance users become addicted, whereas some percent use and remain abuse- and addiction-free. Why either outcome occurs is not known for sure. What is clear, however, is that blaming the addict for addiction is not helpful. It only makes the pain of addiction worse. Compassion for becoming compulsively dependent on a self-destructive substance for survival is what the person needs, not judgmental anger for an outcome he or she did not predict.

Once addicted, people make choices about subsequent use. Although not responsible for his or her condition of addiction, the young person must be held accountable for further use. A boy, for example, whose "kicker" friends all carry containers of smokeless tobacco in their hip pockets, starts to dip in high school because it's a cool and manly thing to do. Out of that culture a few years later, he finds himself addicted to this dangerous form of ingesting nicotine. After viewing the white patches inside the dipper's lips, a dentist warns the young man of the risks of spit tobacco— cancer and other diseases of the mouth. Although not at fault for becoming addicted, the young man is now responsible for maintaining or abandoning further use.

How Is Recovery from Addiction Possible?

Some combination of *rewards* from abstinence (feeling better), *penalties* from using (facing harmful consequences), and taking *responsibility* for further choice (owning one's decisions) are what gets a young person sober and into recovery. Thus, parents who blame, rescue, and make excuses for their child often undermine the very outcome they desire.

Strong as it is, the hold of addiction is vulnerable to being broken on at least three counts.

1. *Addiction is not continuous confusion.* There are moments of sobriety where remorse, reflection, and resolve occur. "I'm not spaced out all the time, you know! And when I'm not, sometimes I can see what's happening to me."

2. *Addiction is not completely invasive.* It does not govern all facets of a person's life. A young person's athletic or artistic activities, for example, may suffer little or no interference from the chemical dependency. "An addict is not all I am. There's a lot I do that has nothing to do with that!"

3. *Addiction is not total loss of self-control.* The young person makes choices governing his or her conduct throughout the day, some having to do with substance use. Substance use may influence other choices. Not all his or her daily decisions, however, are drug driven or affected. "Doing drugs isn't always what I decide to do. Plenty of times I could choose to use, but I don't!"

Recovery is possible because although addiction is unchosen, while actively addicted, an individual still has some freedom for independent choice about indulging in, delaying, or abstaining from momentary use, even for seeking help.

Relapse—Two Steps Forward and One Step Back

"How many relapses is it going to take to convince you that you simply can't afford to use at all?"

Good question. For this frustrated parent, whose child has just reappeared from a lost weekend after several months of sobriety, the answer is progress toward recovery is often two steps forward and one step back. Most people are not one-trial learners when it comes to giving up a persistent habit, addiction being one of the most persistent habits of all. Slips and relapses are part of the halting process of recovery—resisting, occasionally succumbing, to the lure of the old substance while struggling to learn and practice how to live drug-free. According to one source: "At least 40 percent of those who seek help will relapse in the first year." (See Suggested Reading, Arterburn and Burns, p. 147.)

Most good treatment programs do not discharge a young person without equipping him or her with two plans: one to support recovery and another to protect against the possibility of relapse. Critical to maintaining sobriety is knowing, for example, what situations, relationships, experiences, and cues to avoid. Advice from three sources on this matter are worth repeating.

1. "Don't get hungry, angry, lonely, or tired." "If you don't want to slip, don't go where it's slippery." (AA)

2. Beware of these trouble signs (see Suggested Reading, Schuckit, pp. 222–224). "You are in trouble when you think you've really got it licked." "You are in trouble when you find yourself interacting with heavy-drinking and drug-using friends." "You are in trouble when you allow the day-to-day life pressures to build up so that old feelings come back again."

3. It is ". . . sometimes necessary to treat depression, which, if left untreated, may lead the patient to relapse. Depression, in my opinion, is the most common cause of relapse or treatment failure." (See Suggested Reading, Phelps and Nourse, p. 234.)

Relapse typically occurs because emotional memories of the addictive high run very deep, and when stimulated can arouse old cravings and compulsions too powerful to resist. Relapse doesn't discount or destroy work done in recovery. Indeed, for many young people, it turns out to be a powerfully convincing experience, causing them to more fully accept the vulnerability of their condition, and to strengthen their commitment to get back on, and stay on, a path of recovery.

32

~~~~~~

RECOVERING TRUSTWORTHY COMMUNICATION

HONESTY INSTEAD OF LYING

Recovery from addiction requires recovering the capacity to tell the truth to oneself and to others. *All addiction depends on lying. All recovery depends on honesty.* The solution is that easy, and that hard.

Substance-abusing and addicted young people come to depend on lying to get away with their illicit use. Aware of doing the forbidden and living in fear of discovery, they deny, cover up, and create elaborate fictions to conceal the truth. To the frustration and bewilderment of parents, they pretend and promise that all is well in spite of powerful evidence to the contrary.

"We keep being told nothing's the matter, when we know that something is wrong. Our child is acting like a different person. Which are we to believe: what we're told or what we see?" *When words and actions do not match, put your trust in actions.* Then, directly address the issue of dishonesty with the child.

The High Costs of Lying

Although parents cannot force their substance-abusing or dependent child to tell the truth, they can apply consequences when lying occurs, describe how it feels to be lied to, and sit down with the boy or girl and enumerate the high costs of lying.

1. *Liars confuse other people* who don't know what to believe. "Are you telling us you weren't at the party even though other people say you were?"

2. *Liars exploit other people* by taking advantage of their trust. "Of course we believed you, you're our child aren't you?"

3. *Liars injure those they love.* "We feel so hurt you haven't trusted us with the truth."

4. *Liars borrow trouble*, buying freedom with lies now, hoping truth won't come due later. "Didn't you know that at some point we'd find out?"

5. *Liars are double punished* for doing wrong and then denying it. "We're talking about two sets of consequences—one for the offense and another for lying about it."

6. *Liars lead a double life*, mixing truth with fiction and losing track of which is which. "First you said you didn't know anything about it, and now you're telling us you did."

7. *Liars live in fear* of being found out. "You act like you're afraid of being around us, why?"

8. *Liars lack courage to face the truth.* "Don't you ever wish you had what it takes to be honest?"

9. *Liars feel out of control*, telling more lies to cover up the ones they've already told. "Your story is getting more and more unbelievable."

10. *Liars lower their self-esteem*, lacking the capacity to confront the reality of what is going on. "Why don't you just have the courage to admit what you did?"

11. *Liars are misunderstood* because they create a false impression others think is real. "We were just responding to you based on what you told us."

12. *Liars are hard to trust* because they have lied so often before. "Why should we believe you now?"

13. *Liars are lonely people.* "How can we feel close if we can't trust you to be honest?"

14. *Liars fool themselves* by coming to believe some of their own lies. "You're treating what didn't really happen as if it did."

15. *Liars feel guilty* for hurting those they love. "If you feel so badly about yourself for lying to us, why do you do it?"

16. *Liars live in a hostile world*, reaping anger from the victims of their lies. "We resent being lied to all the time."

17. *Liars are usually relieved to be found out* because there's no need to live in hiding anymore. "It's much more relaxing to be open, accurate, and unguarded about what you say."

18. *Liars discover the truth about lying.* It is far less stressful to be the person lied to than the person who must live by telling lies. "Being honest means feeling free to be true to yourself and to others."

Managing to Tell the Truth

Lying to get, or to get away with, something now creates psychological expenses that sooner or later must be paid. Therefore, if parents catch their son or daughter continually being dishonest instead of speaking the truth, they might want to help the child reckon the many costs listed above.

In addition, they can let the child know that they will treat dishonesty as a significant offense. For every lie that is told, that they catch, there will be a task assigned around the home, in addition to regular chores, to be done. Why? To send this message: "We hope this consequence will remind you that for the sake of family intimacy, trust, and safety, we must have the truth between us."

After the infraction is worked off, then parental trust needs to be reinstated because *the healthy expectation for honesty must prevail.* For parents to say, as is tempting, "We're not going to trust you for a long time," is damaging on two counts. It can encourage the child to keep lying: "Why should I tell you the truth if you're not going to believe me?" And it can drive parents crazy with suspicion: "To keep acting like we can't trust you is keeping us awake at night with worry, and we can't emotionally afford to live that way."

33

~~~~~~

RECOVERING PRODUCTIVE COMMUNICATION

DIRECTNESS INSTEAD OF DIVERSION

As substance abuse increasingly preoccupies a young person's life, with the gratification it provides and the problems it creates, conflicts of interest between parents and child typically become more frequent and intense. While the child is pushing against and getting around family restraints to gain freedom to use, parents are pushing back for the sake of safety and responsibility, trying to get a dangerous situation back under control.

By the time that drug involvement has become drug abuse, however, these conflicts often only lead to frustration. Resolution of differences rarely occurs because the process for communicating about disagreements has broken down. "No matter how long we discuss or how hard we argue, we never get anywhere, at least not where we wanted to go. In fact, things just get more and more confused." Exactly. *One hallmark of a young person's substance abuse is increased conflict with parents, with decreased resolution of the differences involved.*

To the extent that the substance-abusing child's behavior creates confusion, crisis, and chaos in the family, the resulting disorganization makes it more difficult for parents to concentrate and act consistently in order to keep a clear focus and a firm family structure in place. The beneficiary of this disorganization is the substance-abusing child. As parents lose hold of what is happening, the young person gets away with more, and conflict settles less and less.

The Tactics of Evasion and Distraction

For parents, the point of this conflict with their child is to resolve an issue by agreeing on a definition of what is or is not going to happen. For the young substance abuser, *evasion* and *distraction* are tactics commonly used to keep parents from reaching this definition point they seek. Consider the following dialogue as an illustration.

The parents say:	*The child responds:*
"You didn't turn in any homework this week." *(specific issue)*	"I'm working much harder, like I promised. Why don't you give me credit for trying?" *(abstract issue)*
"Three teachers I talked to said they asked you for your homework, that you said you'd turn it in, and that you never did." *(accurate statement)*	"You always side with the teachers. You never side with me!" *(extreme statement)*
"What are you going to do to get the overdue homework in?" *(present focus)*	"All you do is bring up the past against me. I'll get it done if you'll just leave me alone!" *(past or future focus)*
"Your job is to get the homework, do it, and turn it in when due." *(expects responsibility)*	"It's not my fault if the teachers can't get me to do the assignments." *(makes excuses)*
"I want a plan for making up your homework." *(declaration)*	"You don't care about my feelings. All you care about is school!" *(manipulation)*

"I intend to keep talking to you about homework until it gets done." *(sticking to the subject)*	"Where's supper? I'm hungry. Why can't we ever eat on time?" *(changing the subject)*

It's like a dance of engagement and avoidance. Parents try to pin their substance-abusing child down while he or she keeps trying to slip away. Unless parents are steadfast in discussing those issues upon which the health and safety of their child depends, they may find the influence they want eroding away. Unable to resist arguing with the diversionary issues that the child keeps raising, parents will get on the defensive, unwittingly following the child everywhere but where they want to go.

Managing Communication Directly

Conflict creates resemblance, with each party tempted to imitate tactics of the other that prove effective. For parents, it is important not to succumb to playing by the substance-abusing child's diversionary rules, but to stand by direct ones of their own. They can encourage their son or daughter to deal with conflict by

- discussing specifics
- making accurate statements
- focusing on the present
- assuming responsibility
- declaring wants
- sticking to the subject

34

▲▲

RECOVERING EFFECTIVE DECISION MAKING

DECLARATION INSTEAD OF MANIPULATION

The deeper into substance involvement a young person sinks, the more urgent it feels to get decisions (to provide money or allow freedom, for example) from parents that will enable his or her drug-using ways. At points of conflict, the boy or girl may first resort to superficial reasoning and relentless argument to prevail: "I keep telling you and telling you, nothing can happen to me from midnight to two that can't happen between ten and midnight, so what's the big deal of my coming in around three? Give me a good reason. You know you can't!" (There are more drinking drivers out later at night, and more alcohol-related car accidents.)

If simple logic, however, does not win out, with parents holding fast to the limit they have set, the young substance abuser may resort to a more powerful kind of persuasion: *emotional extortion*—using the intense expression of emotionality to get parents to relent.

The Tactics of Emotional Extortion
Substance-abusing and addicted young people frequently exploit the power that comes with breaking the code

of conduct other family members typically observe. Lying, stealing, violating agreements, and using profanity and sexually offensive language can create an outlaw presence in the family—someone free to live by his or her own set of rules.

Sigh the parents: "She does what she likes when she likes. And if we cross her, there's no telling how she'll act!"

"So what do you do?"

"Nothing. We tiptoe around her. We give her space or we give her what she asks for. Anything to keep from getting her upset. Anything to keep the peace."

One of the most destructive forms of enabling is when parents fail to make normal demands or set normal limits with their drug-abusing child because they fear the emotional repercussions.

"It's not our fault she's a bully," they explain in their defense.

"It's partly your fault, because there's no such thing as a self-made bully. Bullies are made by their victim's consent. It will take courage, but you need to stop giving her permission to push you around. You only end up empowering her in an unhealthy way when you give in to what you don't want, or back off from what you do. You allow freedoms you believe she shouldn't have."

Bullying itself, however, is only one form of emotional extortion. Parents need to recognize a number of others. Each is an expression of strong emotionality that plays on a particular emotional vulnerability in parents.

- *Love.* By acting appreciative, affectionate, and pleasing, a child can soften up a parent who is vulnerable to needing approval. "How can I refuse him when he's usually so mean, and now he's being so nice?"

- *Anger.* Silently or loudly, a child can communicate irritation or outrage and soften up a parent who is vulnerable to feelings of *rejection.* "I can't stand it when my child accuses me of being unfair or of doing him wrong."

- *Criticism.* Acting dissatisfied with the parent, a child can attack parental character and competence, softening up a parent who is vulnerable to feelings of *inadequacy.* "I can't stand being a failure in my child's eyes."

- *Suffering.* Acting hurt or crying, a child can soften up a parent who is vulnerable to feelings of *guilt.* "I hate feeling responsible for my child's unhappiness."

- *Helplessness.* Acting victim of a parent's decision, a child can communicate resignation and can soften up a parent who is vulnerable to feelings of *pity.* "We hate seeing our child passively surrender to our refusal and just give up."

- *Apathy.* Acting as if the relationship doesn't matter anymore after an unwelcome parental decision, the child can communicate a loss of caring that can soften up a parent who is vulnerable to fear of *abandonment.* "I don't want to make a decision that might cost my relationship with my child."

- *Explosiveness.* Acting as if he or she is going to lose physical control in response to a parental decision, the child can communicate the possibility, or provide an example, of violence that can soften up a parent who is vulnerable to *intimidation.* "I get so scared, I'll do anything so I don't get hurt."

Managing to Be Declarative

A tactic used by many children (and by some adults), emotional extortion is particularly common with young substance abusers who feel driven to get their way at any cost. To stop this manipulation, parents must refuse to play along. They must resist the pull of their own emotional vulnerability (to rejection, guilt, intimidation, and the like) and not let it overrule their judgment and affect their decisions. If they do not, the parental stands they need to take will not hold up, and both they and the child will pay for this infirmity.

The best response to efforts at emotional extortion is for parents to model and insist on *declaration*, refusing to be swayed by this manipulation. Manipulation is about tricking or overpowering the other person to win one's way. Declaration is about each person *proposing specific wants* and then *negotiating a specific resolution* that both parties can agree to accept, sometimes with compromise, sometimes with concession. Manipulation creates distrust and resentment in the party who allows himself or herself to be manipulated, so the manipulator pays a price in ill feelings for the victory he or she has won. Now the relationship is worse off than before. Declaration is about direct communication, respecting what each other has to say, and working out an agreement that works for the relationship.

Thus, when a young substance abuser, bridling at parental restraints and wanting freedom to use, throws a tantrum by combining anger and suffering and explosiveness to maximum manipulative effect, parents must be able to remain rational in the face of this emotional onslaught and declare: "When you can calmly tell us *what it is that you want* or *do not want to have happen*, we will be happy to discuss our decision further. But your acting emotionally upset is *not* going to change our mind."

One final situation, unfortunately, needs to be addressed: what to do when a drug-abusing child threatens physical violence to parents when his or her wants are denied? If parents have previously experienced threats or acts of violence and given in to them to get out of danger, or if they fear that such threats or acts are likely to happen, they should consult with the Juvenile Division of their local police department for advice. Then, they should share that advice with the child so he or she will be fully informed about what they will do should any further threats or acts of violence occur. Sometimes consulting an external social authority is required to enforce a safe situation at home. *Knowing that outside authorities have been informed, and that the eyes of the world are watching, can act as a deterrent to the potentially violent child.*

35

‸‸

RECOVERING MEANINGFUL MUTUALITY

TWO-WAY INSTEAD OF ONE-WAY RELATIONSHIPS

The more extreme that a young person's involvement with substances grows, the more self-centered he or she tends to become. In addiction, for example, the young person compulsively organizes life around one primary objective: to arrange sufficient access to his or her drug of choice. As ministering to this self-destructive habit becomes all-important, the needs of others in the family are increasingly ignored.

"All he thinks about is himself. He doesn't care how his behavior affects the rest of us. We're only good for what we have to give. He won't cooperate unless it gets him what he wants. It's all one-way in the relationship. His needs are all that count. Never ours."

To live primarily on another person's terms, gratifying the young person's wants and needs while having their own neglected in return, parents sooner or later feel exploited and can become resentful: "It's all give and no get, and we're sick of it!"

Beyond this immediate injury to parents, however, there is a serious long-term cost. *Now is later.* How a young person learns to live with family members now is how he or she will live with others later on. And in the long run, one-way relationships don't last very well, be they with friends, fellow employees, roommates, or romantic partners. "If all he wants is a one-way relationship, he can go and live with himself!"

The Meaning of Mutuality

Mutuality means that a relationship is conducted to meet the needs of *both* parties. It is two-way, not one-way, and it requires three levels of exchange.

1. *Reciprocity.* Each party contributes something positive to, and derives something positive from, the relationship.

2. *Compromise.* Each party agrees to sacrifice some self-interest for the sake of the other and for the well-being of the larger relationship.

3. *Sensitivity.* Each party shows consideration for the special needs and vulnerabilities of each other.

As a child gets more and more self-preoccupied with using substances, his or her capacity for mutuality breaks down, and one-way demands increasingly rule the relationship with parents. In terms of reciprocity, the child seems to be saying: "My needs are all that matter." In terms of compromise, the child seems to be saying: "My way is the way it needs to be." In terms of sensitivity, the child seems to be saying: "Only my feelings matter." No wonder parents start feeling resentful.

Managing to Consider Others

For the sake of their immediate well-being with the child, and for the sake of his or her future relationships, parents need to insist on two-way terms—living on terms of mutuality.

179

- To encourage reciprocity, they need to insist on an adequate exchange: "Before we give or do anything you want, you must first give or do something we want for us."

- To encourage compromise, they need to insist on agreement where theirs is not the only self-interest given up: "Before deciding anything, we want you to agree to meet us halfway on whatever arrangement we and you work out."

- To encourage sensitivity, they need to insist that consideration be shown in the relationship: "Before we discuss anything you want, you must demonstrate that you will no longer treat us in hurtful ways."

The quality of family relationships depends, to a large degree, on all parties nurturing the mutuality between them. In recovery, *addicted child and codependent parent need to grow in each other's direction.* The parent needs to become more *self-centered* and insist on the right of mutuality. The child needs to become more *other-sensitive* and accept the responsibility for mutuality. If each can grow toward the other, they can create a healthy relationship that works for them both.

36

RECOVERING
GROWING MATURITY

EFFECTIVE INSTEAD OF INEFFECTIVE
WAYS TO COPE

"I grew up using a lot of drugs," explained a twenty-two-year-old who was trying to get his life back together.

"No you didn't. No one grows up using a lot of drugs, because heavy drug use keeps people from growing up."

As described in Key 2, drug abuse can arrest a child's development because under the influence of substances, he or she frequently disengages from the normal challenges that must be met if growing up is to occur.

- How can a child grow up if unhappy feelings, instead of being faced, are continually escaped?
- How can a child grow up if responsibilities, instead of being met, are continually resisted?
- How can a child grow up if the truth, instead of being told, is continually denied?
- How can a child grow up if work, instead of being accomplished, is continually shunned?
- How can a child grow up if commitments, instead of being honored, are continually broken?
- How can a child grow up if discipline, instead of being developed, is continually neglected?

- How can a child grow up if hard decisions, instead of being made, are continually put off?

Life is just a series of challenges, with the greatest saved for last. People gather maturity by learning to directly engage with the demands that these challenges create, gaining skills of effective coping as they grow. Unfortunately, substance abuse tends to lead the young person off the path of engagement, onto the path of avoidance.

Rather than maturing with every new challenge met, he or she remains immature by choosing "the easy way out," selecting strategies and responses for convenience, not to meet the challenge, but to get around it. In this evasive process, significant opportunity for learning and growth is lost. This is how many young substance abusers actually "outsmart" themselves, winning the battle ("I got away with lying about skipping school") but losing the war ("I finally dropped out because I got so far behind").

Managing to Encourage Maturity

One leadership role of adults is to parent their child (whether substance-using or substance-free) to maturity by encouraging responses that strengthen the young person's capacity to effectively cope with the normal challenges of life. By learning to work problems through to a successful conclusion, the boy or girl increases confidence and capacity in the process. Parents can reinforce mature strategies for coping and discourage those that tend to be immature and less productive.

RESPONSES TO A CHALLENGE

Immature:	or	Mature:
Acting helpless		Acting resourceful
Blaming others		Taking responsibility
Becoming rigid		Being flexible
Acting manipulative		Being declarative
Acting defeatist		Being persistent
Fixating on one choice		Diversifying choices
Acting impulsively		Using restraint
Going to extremes		Using moderation
Distorting reality		Keeping perspective
Demanding one's way		Willing to negotiate
Acting out feelings		Talking out feelings
Shutting down reception		Staying open to listen
Protesting the situation		Solving the situation
Arguing to win		Discussing to understand

Urging mature choices on a child who is abusing substances can be unrewarding for parents to do. If their son or daughter is used to taking the easy way out, he or she may resent and resist their insistence. If they can continually parent their child to maturity, however, parents will give the boy or girl an ongoing opportunity to grow up, even if the child doesn't appreciate this opportunity at the time.

QUESTIONS
AND ANSWERS

How widespread a problem is substance addiction?

The National Institute on Drug Abuse "estimates that 4 million Americans are drug addicts, including 2 million to 3 million hooked on cocaine and 800,000 on heroin. Millions more, though not addicted, use illicit drugs, and 14 million are alcoholics." (*The New York Times*, Science Times, October 27, 1998, p. 1) Notice that this figure does not reflect the number of family members and others whose lives are adversely affected by the addict's self-destructive use.

Is marijuana the gateway drug to other drugs?

In my opinion, there is a gateway drug, but it is not marijuana. It is nicotine, most commonly delivered in the form of cigarettes. Young people who do not smoke have been found to be far less likely to try other drugs and not to become heavy users of alcohol than those who smoked (according to the 1998 National Household Survey on Drug Abuse).

If parents can model not smoking and encourage their child to be a nonsmoker, they may increase the likelihood that he or she will not experiment with other drugs or become seriously involved with alcohol—the most deadly drug of all for young people because of its implication in accidents, injuries, suicides, and other acts of violence.

What about letting our underage child use alcohol at home under parental supervision?

Giving permission to use alcohol at home is giving permission to use substances outside of the home. And it is illegal—just as illegal as if parents hosted a party for their child and served some form of alcohol to his or her underage friends. This is a misdemeanor for which parents can be fined, and should a drunken young guest get hurt or cause harm, parents may be held liable for damages. Laws create many double standards based on age. Voting, driving a car, and consuming alcohol are only a few examples of double standards that discriminate between being an adult and being a child based on the probable capacity to assume significant responsibility. In general, parents should model adherence to the law if they want their child to do the same.

What about parties?

Parties are part of growing up, providing equal parts of social fun and discomfort for most of the young people there. To be invited is to be included. To attend, to some degree, is to pretend—to act like one is enjoying oneself when one may be feeling shy, tongue-tied, awkward, embarrassed, scared, or unsure about what to say, how to respond, or how to fit in. Many grown-ups feel this way at adult parties, too, but they often use alcohol or other substances to lower inhibitions, loosen up, and relax. Children, however, in this socially challenging situation, are expected to remain abstinent, sober, and socially uncomfortable, because they are underage.

Therefore, when *hosting a party* for one's child, parents need to make some arrangements and set some rules.

- No alcohol or other drugs will be served or permitted.
- No party crashers are allowed—invited guests only.
- Lots of food and nonalcoholic beverages will be provided.
- Parents will be visibly present and monitor goings-on, being willing to settle things back down if everyone's natural ebullience gets out of bounds, beyond what their

child can control—roughhousing, food fights, prank calls, and the like.

- Diverse recreational activities are available—games and electronic entertainment.
- The party is confined to a specified room or rooms in which guests are to stay.
- No going on walks around the neighborhood.
- Lights stay on, but dim lights are okay.
- There is a firm time when the party ends.

When *sending a child to a party*, the usual checklist applies.

- What assurance can parents be given that there will be no substances available or used?
- Where is it? (address and phone number)
- What are people going to be doing?
- When is it over?
- What adults will be present? (Check if you feel unsure.)
- Who else that your child knows, and you know, is going?
- How will the child get there and back?

A final warning on parents leaving town for the weekend, leaving the teenager(s) in charge of the apartment or house: In general, *don't do it.* Arrange for some adult presence or at least monitoring of the home while you are gone. *Empty home parties* happen all too frequently when parents are away. The temptation to ask a few friends over is too much for many teenagers to resist. Then word gets out, more people show up than were invited, more substances appear on the scene, the host child loses control of the social situation, often the home is damaged, and sometimes neighbors call the police. And when parents return, they feel violated, betrayed, and very angry.

What about partying and drinking?

Ask the child two questions: Despite your wishes, is he or she sometimes at parties where there is drinking? If so, are people using alcohol to party, or are they partying to use alcohol? If people are partying to drink, they are more likely to drink in order to get drunk, and they are more likely to get drunk to freely do what they would not do when sober. In general, advise the child not to go to or stay at gatherings where socializing is being used as an excuse to drink, and there is competition to see who can get most drunk. Then ask: "Do you sometimes feel you have to drink to fit in?" If the answer is "Yes," then say: "Even though I don't want you to drink, if you must, here is how I advise you to safely do it. Stick to beer, at a rate of no more than one beer an hour, with a limit of two for the evening, eating while you drink."

Is there a connection between drug use and violence?

Yes. The police will tell you that a high proportion of auto accidents, incidents of domestic violence, street fights, assaults, rapes, murders, and suicides are alcohol and drug affected. This is why, should a young person commit an act of violence, he or she needs to soberly reflect on the question: "Would you have done this, would this have happened, if you had not been drunk, high, or wasted?" In service of the distorted reality, sense of immediacy, and freedom for abandon that many substances induce, impulse is allowed to rule and acts of violence are committed. When, to kill suffering from despondency over a performance failure or relationship loss, violence is turned upon oneself, this decision is usually drug or alcohol affected. Overdose of substances itself is the most common means chosen for suicide by young people. Given this reality, *if their child is prone to extreme aggressive outbursts or to deep depressive suffering, in addition to*

187

seeking psychological help, clear the home of all weapons and other ready means of destruction, and remove or secure all alcohol and other drugs as well.

Is there a connection between substance use and AIDS?

Yes. A great many people who inject narcotics, like heroin, contract AIDS by sharing needles with someone who is HIV positive or AIDS infected. In addition, the unprotected sexual promiscuity that can accompany heavy drug use, like cocaine for example, can increase the likelihood of HIV or AIDS transmission.

If a child gives up doing schoolwork because of involvement with drugs, will getting him or her off drugs correct the academic problem?

No. Getting off drugs will only create the opportunity to recover ground that has been lost. Depending on how long drugs have been depleting the child's efforts at school, there may be a need for some *supplemental* (remedial/tutorial) *education* to bring the young person's neglected skills back up to grade level. Children who can't catch up are more likely to give up. In addition, supervisory support by parents is essential, helping the child get back into the habit of processing homework and studying for tests. Finally, if these two steps prove insufficient, then an evaluation of possible learning disability may be in order.

Should you take it seriously if a teacher tells you that he or she suspects drug use in your child based on erratic, disruptive, or spaced-out classroom behavior?

Yes. Any teacher willing to put himself or herself at professional risk by delivering such an unpopular message should cause parents to check out the suspicion. A lot of drug use first becomes apparent at school.

Is there any relationship between substance abuse and Attention Deficit/Hyperactivity Disorder (ADHD)?

"If attention deficit disorder is untreated, the risk of alcohol or substance abuse . . . may be higher among people with this disorder than among those in the general population." (See Suggested Reading, Merck, p. 1253.) Why? The causes are yet to be determined. Perhaps these children (who are often characterized by high impulsivity, extreme distractibility, conflict and excitement-driven behavior, unable to pay and get enough attention) are relying on this self-medication in two possible ways.

1. Using drugs to satisfy their need for high stimulation

2. Using recreational drugs to relieve tension and fatigue from overstimulation so they can relax

Instead of trying to alter their innate brain chemistry by self-medicating, however, they are better served by getting prescription help (if deemed appropriate) from a qualified psychiatrist. According to *The New York Times* (January 28, 1999, p.1) over three million children are now estimated to be taking Ritalin, a psychostimulant, to calm them down, and the number is rising.

These children also often benefit from psychological help to learn how to live within themselves, with others, and with the world in more focused, socially controlled, consistent, effective, organized, and esteem-filling ways. Most important, *if antidepressant medication is prescribed, ADHD children should be told not to use alcohol.* "Excessive drinking in combination with antidepressants is dangerous because the effects of alcohol are intensified . . . The combination of higher doses of antidepressants . . . and excessive alcohol have the greatest potential for causing an accidental overdose." (See Suggested Readings, Zeigler Dendy, pp. 170–171.) *Because of their higher susceptibility to substance abuse when untreated and because of often being prescribed psychoactive medication, ADD and ADHD children should be warned away from recreational drug use.*

How important to having drug-free kids is those kids having drug-free parents?

One source (see Suggested Reading, Arterburn and Burns, p. 181) answers that question this way. "Drug-proof kids come from drug-free parents. Free yourself and your family. Become willing to do whatever it takes to raise drug-proof children in a drug-saturated society. Life comes with no guarantees, but your actions are the best hope for saving your children from the destruction of alcohol and drugs."

GLOSSARY

Addiction coming to compulsively depend upon a self-destructive habit (involving a substance, activity, or relationship) for survival.

Adolescence the period between when a young person leaves childhood, around the age of puberty, and finally grows up enough to accept young adult responsibilities for independence, eight to twelve years later.

Codependency when one person takes responsibility for fixing another person's substance abuse or addiction, and sacrifices personal well-being trying to change what he or she cannot control.

Denial convincing oneself that what has happened, is happening, or is going to happen did not, is not, or will not happen.

Enabling helping to protect someone from the hurtful consequences of his or her destructive choices, so he or she just keeps engaging in problem-causing behavior.

Felony an act of breaking the law that may be punishable by imprisonment or even death.

Intoxication to ingest a substance that excites the body to the point that physical and mental control is diminished.

Misdemeanor an act of breaking the law, not usually punishable by imprisonment.

Recovery the process through which a substance abuser or addict learns to live within himself or herself, with other people, and with the world in a healthy and rewarding drug-free way.

Relapse resuming substance abuse after drugs or alcohol have been given up.

Withdrawal discomfort that happens in the body after drugs that it has grown used to have been taken away.

SUGGESTED READING

Arterburn, Stephen and Jim Burns. *Drug-Proof Your Kids.* Pomona, California: Focus on the Family Publishing, 1989.

Beattie, M. *Co-Dependent No More.* New York: Harper/Hazelden, 1987.

Beck, Aaron T., M.D. *Depression.* Philadelphia: University of Pennsylvania Press, 1970. (Sixteenth printing, 1996.)

Fassler, David G., M.D. and Lynne S. Dumas. *"Help Me, I'm Sad."* New York: Viking Penguin, 1997.

Heller, Richard F., M.D. and Rachael F. Heller, M.D. *Carbohydrate Addicted Kids.* New York: HarperCollins, 1997.

Leite, John S., Ph.D. and J. Kip Parrish, Ph.D. *Successful Parenting.* Deerfield Beach, Florida: Health Communications, 1991.

Merck Research Laboratories. *The Merck Manual of Medical Information.* West Point, Pennsylvania: The Merck Manuals Department, 1997.

Peterson, C., S. Maier, and M. Seligman. *Learned Helplessness.* New York: Oxford, 1993.

Phelps, Janice Keller, M.D. and Alan E. Nourse, M.D. *The Hidden Addiction and How to Get Free.* Boston: Little, Brown & Company, 1986.

Pickhardt, Carl E. *Keys to Parenting the Only Child.* Hauppauge, New York: Barron's Educational Series, Inc., 1997.

—. *Keys to Single Parenting.* Hauppauge, New York: Barron's Educational Series, Inc., 1996.

—. *Keys to Successful Stepfathering.* Hauppauge, New York: Barron's Educational Series, Inc., 1997.

—. *Parenting the Teenager.* P.O. Box 50022, Austin, Texas 78763, 1983.

—. *The Case of the Scary Divorce*. Washington, D.C.: Magination Press, The American Psychological Association, 1997.

Schaefer, Charles E., Ph.D., and Howard L., Millman, Ph.D. *How to Help Children with Common Problems*. St. Louis, Missouri: Plume, 1992.

Schor, Edward L., M.D., ed. *Caring for Your School-Age Child*. New York: Bantam Books, 1997.

Schuckit, Marc Alan, M.D. *Educating Yourself About Alcohol and Drugs*. New York and London: Plenum Press, 1995.

Steinberg, Laurence, Ph.D. and Ann Levine. *You & Your Adolescent*. New York: Harper & Row Publishers, 1990.

Woititz, Janet Geringer. *Adult Children of Alcoholics*. Deerfield Beach, Florida: Health Communications, Inc., 1983.

Zeigler Dendy, Chris A., M.S. *Teenagers with ADD, a Parents' Guide*. Bethesda, Maryland: Woodbine House, 1995.

SUPPORT GROUPS

For recovery assistance from **Alcoholics Anonymous, Al-Anon, Cocaine Anonymous,** or **Narcotics Anonymous,** consult your phone directory for the local numbers.

For information on drug abuse prevention, call: (800) 729-6686, **National Clearing House for Alcohol and Drug Information;** (800) NCA-CALL, **National Council on Alcoholism and Drug Dependence.**

For parental support from **Parents Anonymous** or **ToughLove,** consult your phone directory for the local numbers.

For referrals, call: (800) 853-7867, **Parents' Resource Institute for Drug Education (PRIDE).**

For information and referrals, call: (800) HELP-111, **The National Substance Abuse Hotline.**

INDEX